P[illegible]
Swe[illegible]

'There are few writers I trust [illegible] with the care, nuance and sharp edge that Mad[illegible] *Sweet Nothings.* This book questions what it means to love, to des[illegible] and to reckon with our autonomy in ways that I believe will resonate with all women. A must read from one of Australia's strongest feminist voices.'
Hannah Ferguson, author of *Taboo*

'A courageous interrogation of problematic sex delivered with poetic flourish.' **Chanel Contos, author of *Consent Laid Bare***

'An examination of power and sex that prompts fury for what is done and grief for what is lost.' **Clementine Ford, author of *I Don't***

'With quiet fury and lyric force, *Sweet Nothings* lays bare the shrouded space where pedagogy and power entangle. Griffiths reminds us that women go to university to study—not to become an object of desire.' **Lucinda 'Froomes' Price, author of *All I Ever Wanted Was to Be Hot***

'This is creative non-fiction as its very best—novelistic, poetic, tender and truthful in equal measure. Madison's stunningly beautiful prose is the perfect vessel for these important, intricate stories of desire and power, and this book is profoundly urgent and necessary for our time. Everyone must read this brilliantly rendered, fiercely honest book. The very best non-fiction writing is both hard-hitting and tender, and this book is both of those things and more.' **Lucia Osborne-Crowley, author of *I Chose Elena***

Praise for *Tissue*

'Fierce, poetic and unflinching, Griffiths pulls no punches as she explores what it looks like to find and honour your agency.' **Lucinda 'Froomes' Price, author of *All I Ever Wanted Was to Be Hot***

'At its heart, *Tissue* is a book about selfhood, and all of the decisions that we make, or attempt to make, in order to become ourselves. It is about the stories and forces that attempt to limit this—especially those surrounding gender and sexuality—and how the choice to end a pregnancy might force a reckoning with them. Griffiths' essays are wide-ranging, defiant and impassioned, and incredibly current too.' **Fiona Wright, author of *The World Was Whole***

'A sincere book that curiously and compassionately makes a compelling case for love and choice.' **Gina Rushton, author of *The Most Important Job in the World***

'in language both tender and raw, she imaginatively examines herself, the complexity of her responses … society, sexuality, family and gender with remarkable honesty' ***The Age***

'With smart, beautifully written discussion, Griffiths lays bare the discourse of privilege and choice, addressing what it is to go up against the cultural expectations and condemnations put to those who exercise their human right to choose.' ***Books+Publishing***

'Griffiths writes with literary flourish as she unpicks ideas around gender, femininity, guilt and motherhood.' ***The Guardian***

SWEET NOTHINGS

Also by Madison Griffiths

Tissue

SWEET NOTHINGS

Madison Griffiths

ultimo press

While this is a work of non-fiction, elements of these stories have been changed or fictionalised to preserve anonymity.

ultimo press

Published in 2025 by Ultimo Press,
an imprint of Hardie Grant Publishing

Ultimo Press
Gadigal Country
7, 45 Jones Street
Ultimo, NSW 2007
ultimopress.com.au

ultimopress

A catalogue record for this work is available from the National Library of Australia

Sweet Nothings
ISBN 978 1 76115 185 9 (paperback)

Cover design Mika Tabata
Cover photograph Harvard University, Cambridge, Massachusetts, USA by Monica Garcia / Getty Images
Cover illustration Madison Griffiths
Author photograph Courtesy of Athina Wilson
Typesetting Kirby Jones | 13/23 pt Adobe Garamond Pro
Copyeditor Elena Gomez
Proofreader Ellen O'Brien

10 9 8 7 6 5 4 3 2 1

Printed in Australia by Opus Group, an Accredited ISO AS/NZS 14001 Environmental Management System printer.

MIX
Paper | Supporting responsible forestry
FSC® C018684

The paper this book is printed on is certified against the Forest Stewardship Council® Standards. Griffin Press – a member of the Opus Group – holds chain of custody certification SCS-COC-001185. FSC® promotes environmentally responsible, socially beneficial and economically viable management of the world's forests.

Ultimo Press acknowledges the Traditional Owners of the Country on which we work, the Gadigal People of the Eora Nation and the Wurundjeri People of the Kulin Nation, and recognises their continuing connection to the land, waters and culture. We pay our respects to their Elders past and present.

For Kelly

AUTHOR'S NOTE

It begins with a curiosity worth sweating over. In my late teens, I was once a man's student. In my early twenties, his lover. In my early thirties, a thorn in his side. I had discovered, over the span of a decade, that there had been others he had loved, or at least held: a small handful of students-turned-lovers. At what point was the cushion he'd offered all those years ago, seized from beneath my side and inscribed with somebody else's initials and student number, and then done so a third time? I mulled over the sense of betrayal I bore. Suspicious, not of whether or not love can draw an honest breath in relationships between university staff and students. No, because I had felt it before, big and full. I was suspicious instead of whether or not it was a love worth defending, both institutionally and socially, given how it left me. Bitter, and confused. What are its consequences?

This was when I began posting call-outs online, curious if others could help me trace the silhouette of an ugly, barren feeling. I asked: Have you ever been in a 'pedagogical relationship'? As in, have you ever dated your teacher, tutor, professor or student? I received hundreds of responses: girls who had once harboured crushes on their high school teachers, professors who had curbed the appetites of their students, the children of parents who had met in the classroom, women lit up with pity and the sobering nostrum of age, men turned-on by the tendrils of a clichéd taboo. Of those hundreds, I met Blaine, Elsie, Cara and Rose. Four tangled accounts of power, lust and learning, to each of which I felt an immediate, unshakable pull.

I called my publisher, Brigid, one afternoon a year ago, during the earliest iterations of *Sweet Nothings*, and made obvious my want to look for something previously undetectable in an otherwise run-of-the-mill story. I didn't care to stop and start in the classroom. I wanted to know how gender had found itself decanted into a clean, siphoned-off glass, how the women whose stories I laboured over had had their womanhood marked, time and time again. How they long lived in the particulars of sex and its clumsiness. I didn't necessarily care for scandal, but instead how women find themselves placed in the ruckus of power, desire and surrender. How are our wants, our yearnings, formed in a society littered with sexism?

It must be noted: I have fictionalised elements of each of their stories, as well as assigned each person I mention in *Sweet Nothings* a pseudonym. I have done this to preserve their anonymity. Throughout the span of my research, I also found myself deliberating over acts of non-consent, relationships between high-school students and their teachers, and pornography. It started to appear obvious to me that sex between university students and their superiors felt contaminated by larger, more damning forces. Yes, there is more corrupting abuse that occurs, particularly when a high-school teacher makes an advent calendar out of his student's proximity to her eighteenth birthday. There appears a vacuum of misogyny both in—and outside—of the classroom, that relies heavily on the erotic outline of teacher–student relationships, both within—or without—the legal or moral parameters of acceptance. I felt it remiss to not scrutinise my surroundings a little, just to see what remained.

I also refrain from differentiating between tutors and professors. While I acknowledge the gulf of power that exists between these two professional markers in most disciplines, particularly when it comes to financial and material authority, I was eager to centre the testimony of students and their place in the sexual economy of academic institutions. After all, students look towards a singular beacon of guidance, and in many cases their tutors—the ones who dated or slept with their students—did not suddenly abstain from doing so, come their professorship.

This book relies, in its interrogation, on the same stock-standard modes of gender it critiques, which is why I have chosen to focus primarily on female students and their relationships with male professors and tutors. This felt important, largely due to its commonness. I take these relationships to be a gendered phenomenon. In them, we are never far from the jejune conspiracy of sex and power, of the trite and stale need to make 'woman' their subjects. In a lot of ways, it is this discovery that saturated my sense of betrayal. Here, I felt made 'woman', in all of the ways I resented.

1

In her courtyard, Rose is pulling the brittle heads of dead blooms from their stalks. She does this with her left hand, as she holds her phone to her ear with her right. Apoplectic with a new kind of rage, she is: pacing about barefoot on the hot concrete of her backyard as her cat peers curiously out the window at her, making note of her movements. Rose knows that—if she can help it—this will, very likely, be the last time she will speak to Samuel. The quake in her voice thrums bravely, as if now home to something animal, biting. A sad, sentient oaf of a thing, forcing her to give in to its own rigorous pulse, to the knee-jerk mechanics of breath, and spit, and sting. As if, right then, it knew something she didn't. Or, worse: it knew something she too had always known, which defeated her even more, the truth of him and her so obvious, so plain. So damn unbecoming.

'I called him a pervert,' she laughs, a little riled as she repeats aloud her chosen poison to me. 'Can you believe that? A fucking pervert.'

I have surrendered to my desires before. I have placed myself squarely in the eyeline of something fierce and rule-less: a kiss when there shouldn't have been one, refuge in the wrong person's sweat. I try to remind myself of this before every interview I conduct as research for this book. I don't want to be careless or judgemental. How tempting it would be to lean on lazy, hardened scripts. Run-of-the-mill stories about horny professors, the precocious students they want to hold and the negligence of the institutions they play in. Academic operators who tend to decide, rather hopelessly, how best to tame the garden of weeds they've long sown. I imagine a cartoon rendering of the University of Melbourne shrugging, before saying, in a goofy, old-timey voice: 'All right, folks! Do we douse our plot in water when nobody's looking and act astonished—bewildered, even!—when it grows awry?' Or perhaps something less believable: 'Do we rip it up and start again?'

Rose is twenty-eight years old when she finds out. That same week, she runs a red light, and the eerie resounding of a tram's *ding*—the one that nearly nicked the backside of her car—leaves her feeling funny. She picks a fight with a man outside a pub, in defence of somebody else, just because. She peels her degree from the underbelly of a forgotten box that lives in her garage, barricaded by cobwebs and the spiders who spun them, and counts its paper creases. She combs through a decade-long archive of Facebook messages, screenshots a few, and assembles them together in a pitiful folder of boring affidavits, titling it, Samuel. And then there are the grossly off-kilter things she does as well, when nobody is around. Like early in the morning, when she presses her eyes firmly together, her fingers traversing about regretfully beneath her underwear. It is then that she pictures him in class, gesticulating with his slender hands. Her mouth slightly ajar when—in her fantasy—he homes in on a pretty blonde with a slight smile and an open notepad, and holds her gaze for a moment longer than the others, longer even than Rose's, until she keels forward in climax. Sometimes, after this lonely ritual, and just before catching her breath, she feels as if she might cry. Might let out a dusty excuse of a wail. But she never does.

Desire, and the collateral damage that ensues. Perhaps that is what this story is about. I have conducted many interviews, with many former students. I have listened as each has chosen to unfurl their teacher-turned-lover's desire, to show me where it starts and ends. To hold it up, as if it is a map of the universe, and they are an eager child gripping a worn crayon, scribbling a chalky line between each planet as it orbits slowly around a greedy sun, only to eventually say to me, 'You see that one? With its dints, and orbs? Yes, that one was me.' For Rose, she was the first. Three years into her relationship with Samuel, there were rumours of another. Just last month, a third. Three strikes. Too big, too blatant, for Rose to forgive. He had told her in their last conversation, perhaps foolishly, that he didn't realise this would affect her as much as it had, 'this' being a long-standing proclivity to fall for former students. In a lot of ways, she hadn't imagined it would either. Can one ever anticipate being made a notch on somebody else's bedpost?

I was quick to look up Samuel's name online. He was polished, despite dressing a little offbeat. He had black, tapered eyebrows, nice lips, a keen stare. Hardly eager to please. I had a ferocious impulse to reach out and introduce myself to him. I wanted to ask him if he ever found himself surprised—embarrassed, even—by his tendencies, if they rippled through him softly come the start of semester, come always, or whacked him sore if, and only if, a particular student caught his eye. I wanted to ask him if desire had jostled him stupid, steered him off course. If he thought himself a fool, or worse, the opposite: a man shamelessly aware of his power and just how to wield it. And then what would I decide? Why did I think it mattered how an impulse as reckless and clichéd as this found him—be it hunched and sorry, or boastful and heady—and whether it left him, when or if it did, in much the same way? You see, I also wonder about my own proclivities, in a way that any good writer hellbent on understanding her subjects ought to. Why did I fly to Brisbane that time, in 2019, to meet a man

I rolled around with for five short days, a man I barely knew, who admitted to me once—between hot tears—that he had smacked his ex-girlfriend across the cheek? How did I, a few years later, manage to fall asleep in an unfamiliar bed, enveloped in the embrace of an unfamiliar body, as my then-boyfriend waited, with resolute breath, for a text back, querying why I wasn't home yet? 'Why am I like this?' we all ask ourselves, in those nasty, barren moments, when lust and lechery make us screw up our sad, strange faces, and hand us the tools to vandalise the walls we long laboured over, the ones we hoped would keep us warm.

Sometimes, and only if excited or frenzied or a little drunk, Rose's accent errs into shrill, ocker lyricism. This, among other things, is what attracts me to her. And her to me, I think, as if somewhere along the way she managed to figure me out, decided that I too had wriggled my way out of a small, plodding town on the outskirts of Melbourne, and that my mother likely cried when I did. Her anger is hardly civilised. It escapes her often, veiling itself in snide, ugly quips. Like the time she harangued a friend-of-a-friend in the third aisle at her local Coles, and—with a dastardly smile on her face—took his pleasantries ('How have you been? What's been going on?') as permission to wallow, to divulge. Him, with a sympathy that had long expired by the time Rose took it upon herself to relay to him the best bits. The more indifferent he became, the faster she got. She catalogued Samuel's actions in swift, serrated order, until he halted her crudely with a simple, fixed glance at his phone. Perhaps it was hardly crude at all, and he was simply eager to finish assembling together his groceries. Rose smiled before complimenting his sneakers, and hurtled feverishly towards the check-out, embarrassed.

She wasn't always angry, but now she is. On that last phone call with Samuel, he sounded almost exactly like the man she had loved for four big years, only colder. When he answered, she didn't trip on her words. She asked him if it was true, what she had heard. If he could tell her the facts of the matter: that yes, he had fallen in love with another former student. If they were back here again, never far from the wounded truth of it all. But then again, he didn't trip on his words either, as if she were an omen he had prepared himself to meet one day, a symptom of something larger, more dreadful.

Unlike Rose, I never told the man whose undoing I hoped to orchestrate just how and when I'd do it. A hot-tempered ex-boyfriend, hardly deserving of notice. I quoted him tirelessly in articles, imploring the world read about his abuse, trussing it into sentences and pitching his confessions to editors instead. I never heard him react, or fumble his way through a filthy remark, or hurl rage at me over phone static. But Rose wanted something else from Samuel. She needed him to know that she saw him. That, *yes, unlike your current girlfriend, who fawns over how you caress your neat, nice chin while looking her squarely in both eyes as she speaks, I see you.*

Blaine is different. An academic bordering on forty, she is hardly gung-ho, has tucked her anger into someplace tiny, someplace hidden, and refrained from peering inside. Greg noticed her close to two decades ago, with her neat, thick fringe and fastidious eyes, meandering through the leafy, campus quadrangle between his classes. Blaine is beautiful, but hardly aware of it. I feel compelled to tell her. As if I need to correct some egregious wrong. She blushes, like I am the first person to ever say so. Growing up, there are the girls who know and the girls who don't—and the girls who do very quickly become experts in being looked at, peered into, fiddled with. Friends of their fathers will insist they perch up on the worn denim of their laps and smile. Boys will wait for the lights to dim, or for the sparkling wine to slur their speech, before planting a hot kiss on their cheek, or lips, or the back of their necks if they are already asleep. Lip gloss and cheap polyester thongs are stolen from department stores and tucked into the bottom of schoolbags. The hungry once-overs of men—often twice or thrice their age—who wait opposite them by the footpath are carved into their young minds. Blaine, insecure instead, never anticipated her body as a kind of spell able to be summoned out from beneath its cotton. Never considered it the kind of thing men pined after. Least of all her professor.

She doesn't tell anybody the first time it happens. Or the fifth, or the twentieth. The first kiss arrives as if on the coat-tails of the ocean breeze near Riverside Drive, unexpected and brisk. They meet at a garish sports bar in the heart of the city, under the guise of academic camaraderie, Blaine having just commenced her PhD in the same department Greg had long soured in, his indignation obvious and sharp.

She finishes her riesling, and he orders her another, insistent that they stay long enough to sip on a couple of dessert wines. 'The night is young,' he says, smiling, and so is she. So clever, so wise beyond her years, so able to keep up.

The port is buttery and rich, and Blaine is a little tipsy. She giggles at a troupe of rowdy men nearby, lobbing their fists in the air towards the television. On the screen, larger men can be seen caving in on each other and themselves, adorning their opposition in mud and blood with every hard, blistering tackle. She does not envy their wives or girlfriends, these men. How uninspiring, to have their husbands belch and swear and spit and snore, the kind of geezers insistent on a cleanly shaven pussy and cleaner again linen. They remind her of the boys she grew up with, who would appear, post summer holidays, rattled and raucous in the schoolyard, their faces a little diced from blowing up gunpowder for shits and giggles in their father's sheds. Greg winks at her, as if to say that he agrees. That yes, these men are rudimentary, gross. That perhaps they should get out of this godforsaken jungle, a place that reeks of violence and spilt tinnies. Then, a stone's throw from the pub, he pulls her in at the waist and kisses her.

When I mention to strangers that I'm working on this book, they want to know where my interest lies. On whose bed did the original curiosity transpire, and which professor was it? Which don at what institution knows how it feels to caress my hips, and thighs, and cheeks with his fingers, to lock eyes with me in the mirror above a washbasin as the two of us clean our teeth of a morning, or argue over which takeaway joint to sink our pay cheque into of an eve, long after the essay has been graded and attendance has been checked? *Why else*, I feel their eager faces insinuating, *would you care?*

While writing this book, I meet an obnoxious handful of socialites on one particular night out, the kind who insist on asking to see everybody's handle before anything else, only to punch it into their search bar, scroll zealously through a stockpile of mutuals, and point out which ones they've fucked, collaborated with, or just happen to hate a little. One of them, Liam, is an aspiring director with a greasy ponytail.

'What do you do?' Liam asks me, jittery. I tell him I'm a writer working on my second book, and he asks what it is about. I start with a poky, pared-back synopsis: something about it being a musing on university professors and the students some of them choose to sleep with, to love. 'Wow,' he begins. He then proceeds to ask why I care to interrogate this, and—well before I have the chance to answer—he shrugs, lifting his sweaty palms from his knees, and boorishly declares, 'I'm not suggesting you were raped by a professor, if that's what you think.' I look askance at Liam, unsure how best to respond. It is then that I decide not to muddy the waters with my own chronicle, lest it distract others. I will tiptoe around it instead, and even pretend to have never been nineteen, to have never clutched my tutorial readings and held them to my chest excitedly, as if they—like he, who administered said readings—had a spine and ribs and lips I cared to feel.

Oh, how people become wrapped up in the physicality of these relationships, in the viscera. This, they imagine, is where and how it tumbles into badness: a stolen kiss, the unfastening of belts or loosening of ties, the fumbling of pants that end up splayed by the bedside in a scandalous heap, or—as Liam crows—a rape, a violation as glaring as it is ancient. So obvious, so unforgiving. As children, if we are fortunate enough, we learn of touch and all of its ensuing dangers abstractly, and only by being taught how *not* to touch: be it by pressing too tightly, or pushing too clumsily. Prisoners to our own curiosity. We will eagerly pinch together the wings of a cabbage moth in our mothers' gardens, only to have an adult spell out our crimes to us once the damage is done, once we appear before a parent, elated. We'll stand, holding up our hands to reveal the floury evidence of having fondled the body of something far smaller and weaker than ourselves. But the creature does not die, as the old allegory goes. Instead, her colours and patterns may temper, making her more susceptible to peril. Is he who kills the bug the one who left thumbprints in her wings that time, or the wasp who notices her later, long after a tiny vandalism has taken place, her scales barely able to help her shield herself from danger? I consider Liam's curiosity hardly novel, or interesting. If we are to imagine a sexual scandal, we conjure an image of it at its most grotesque. We are to hope, if anything, that it be imbued with torment and greed, with many a half-wet kiss from an older man on the soft, chaste lips of a younger woman. We, too, ache to be held back after class, if only just to see.

I think this is why I felt pulled to Cara. 'Madison,' she exhales in one of our many phone calls, 'nothing happened. You see, it was all very gentle, which is why I can't understand you wanting to speak to me.' In the evenings, she flicks on all of the lamps in her apartment's lounge, loosens her hair, and pours herself a glass of shiraz. It is then that she plays solitaire alone, quietly dealing herself thirteen piles. Eight years earlier, her nights were occupied elsewhere: slumped atop her tutor Ivan's throw blanket as he fingered nobly through a book nearby, reciting sentences about art in our current geological age, abased landscapes. About just what it means to be carrying on, to be tap dancing around a drawn-out environmental collapse. She cannot count how many evenings she spent on his bed, in his quaint Clifton Hill flat, her body inches from his. There had been months and months of capricious emails. 'Here's an article I read recently,' he'd offer. A link to a timely essay paired with a small, definitive statement. 'How curious,' he'd state, and then there'd be something else, 1000 more words—from *The New Yorker*, or an esoteric academic journal—for Cara to devour. But he never laid a hand on her, not once.

A female scholar I interview, who specialises in romance theory, finds this arrangement curious but hardly reputable. 'The absence of touch is a lie he can tell himself,' she offers, unfavourably. Eight years ago, in the Clifton Hill flat, Cara notes how Ivan lights a small family of candles. She watches him in silence as he hovers his lighter atop the wax vertebrae of his bedroom. This, she explains to me now, is their ritual. She sinks into the warmth of his quilt, her face flushed, and he kickstarts their twice-weekly routine: caressing all the crude, soft parts of her mind by way of words alone. She does not stay the night. She never does. But as she roams back home, towards the nearby apartment she shares with her sister, she lets her mind wander to the untoward areas, the ones he keeps at an arm's length. The untouchable parts. This is how she does it: she sucks the juice from their cerebral bond, knowing it will never sour.

2

Women talk. Rose knows this, and so does Ellen, who dials Rose's number on that fateful December morning after attending a conference with Samuel and submits her findings. Rose and Ellen had met through him five years ago. Ellen was an honours student in Samuel's department, a handful of years younger than Rose. This shared settlement, a contract of noticing, is hardly fixed, but a dotted line seems to materialise nonetheless, a roped thing that fetters both parties together at the wrists and forces their hand in signatories.

Samuel and Ellen had, once upon a time, established a close friendship. Together, they forged a terrific weekend repertoire: her and him, hopping between Ubers and slinking through the back entrances of terrace houses, where one of many grubby parties ensued. Rose was initially thrown off-balance by Ellen and Samuel's newfound connection, distracted only by Ellen's age and something she would later identify as a terribly inconvenient hunch: a suspicion that, perhaps, she ought to be wary of Samuel's heed for intelligent female students, especially those quite a bit younger than him. Women relatively similar—but, in a lot of ways, different—from her. Her inkling made itself known a year into the two of them living together. Before noon, Samuel would peel his laptop open, pour himself a coffee, and commence teaching, while Rose stirred awake in their nearby bed. First, he would clear his throat. Then, he'd begin by addressing the pixelated display of young hopefuls before him, his voice stern but playful. Rose hated how often she'd find herself wincing, frustrated.

She describes his cadence to me now. It is like she is an unforgiving sleuth: a detective who has long played in the silky gutter of somebody else's oesophagus, who points out each swallow, each pause, as if it is a conspiracy or sign.

I can't blame her. Those same intonations captivated her once. Perhaps they even masqueraded as foreplay. There was a time, many years ago, that they held her heart hostage. For twelve beautiful weeks, she hung on to every word—a rhythm, merciless and magnificent, the same one that carried her here, to the warmth of their shared bed. I think she would've loved him to reposition his desktop monitor slightly, just so she could be seen by his cohort. Then, maybe he'd stand from his desk, flip her tired body around and reveal the white, wet underbelly of their love, allowing her to mark her territory in the hot arrow of his students' eyeline.

But Ellen wasn't a threat. She was fun, shrewd and hardly impressionable. It was almost as if Samuel had to earn Ellen's attention, not the other way around. Rose liked that. Ellen was also the only friend of Samuel's who maintained a friendship with Rose, long after the break-up. Everybody else had become distant, snide, so much so that if Rose were to bump into any of Samuel's friends down the street, they'd blush and strut off. Rose hated being disliked, but she hated any kind of head-to-head even more than that, so each time it happened she would just patch together a smile and leave.

In December, Ellen attends a conference. Dowdy philosophers gather in lecture theatres after months of anchoring themselves to abstruse theories, and do their best to wheedle their chosen topics into small talk. Both Samuel and Ellen are in attendance, but neither are presenting, deciding instead to drift in and out of a number of sessions and to meet later for drinks. At the pub, though, Samuel appears distracted. Ellen finds this surprising, particularly given she has brought Melanie along, a willowy, blonde friend of hers working in the area of virtue ethics, whom Samuel has long tried to charm. Not only is Samuel distracted, he seems more elated than usual, abundantly confident.

'Are you seeing anybody?' Ellen asks him when he checks his phone for a fourth time.

'What? Oh, no. Not at the moment,' he responds, before insisting the next round is on him. He collects a jug, and as his hands are busy pouring three pints, his phone—now laying face-up on the timber bench—vibrates. A name, littered with kitsch emojis, appears on the screen, and Ellen takes heed.

In retelling this story, Rose stresses to me that Ellen's watchfulness isn't undue, but I'd be lying if I wasn't slightly taken aback. I am curious as to why an adult man, a person Ellen considered a friend at the time, was being surveilled so obviously.

'I hope you're not having too much fun without me,' the text reads, and Samuel, embarrassed, removes his phone from the table and pockets it. Ellen is withdrawn for the remainder of the evening, slotting the occasional yawn into their exchanges. Her eyes now like reticent, all-knowing daggers. Ellen recalls, in that moment, a previous time—say, a month or two before—when Samuel admitted something to her he shouldn't have: that a student of his had become flirtatious, had made quiet, but obvious, advances. Ellen was hardly impressed when he said it, and—not even halfway through such idle gossip—hissed a single laden word. 'Don't.' He floundered a little—'Of course not, I've already drawn a line in the sand!'—but had already mentioned her name, the same name that appeared, just now, in the chassis of love-heart emojis on his lock-screen. 'You stupid, stupid bastard,' she thinks.

That evening, unable to sleep, Ellen looks fixedly at her ceiling. She methodically prepares a small, terrible list in her mind, while her heeler kicks out in his slumber, his warm body nestled at the foot of her bed. If she is to do this, she thinks, she ought to do it properly. The history of her and Samuel's friendship loops, like an unforgiving showreel. It interrupts her thoughts, her procedure. She peels her phone from its charger and makes a note to email Josephine, the head of school. There are others, women with thick-rimmed glasses and wringing hands, who hatch together curriculum and tutoring contracts, that ought to know. And then, of course, there's Rose, who—like Ellen—has long forgiven him, has wiped a stray tear or ten from his cheek. Men like Samuel never seem to learn.

Rose is packing a cone with the shrivelled offcuts of bush weed when Ellen eventually calls the next morning. At first, it is funny. The two laugh riotously, loudly, between peppered jabs. A character assassination ensues, carrying on in full, eager stead. 'He's fucking gone and done it again?' Rose scoffs. It is only once Ellen hangs up that Rose's anger swells, changes. I see her now, fumbling with it. It scales the walls around her like a putrid monkey. A stupid, conniving beast. If ever it notices her starting to loll, to settle, it flings whatever it can find at her, aiming squarely at her small, pretty face. It does not miss. 'Good-for-nothing piece of shit!' it laughs, quoting Ellen. 'I want to hear you say it, Rose!' Bawling. 'Louder! I want him to hear you! Don't you want that? Why don't you want that?'

Women notice. Rose and Ellen's pact is just this: a landmark case of noticing. Samuel had tried his best to hide how he had met Rose from Ellen some years ago, but women notice. Women notice, and then they talk, and then they equip each other in big, burnished suits of armour and report their findings. Perhaps this is why I am taken aback when, after emailing a female researcher based out of Michigan who speaks online about the problematic nature of pedagogical relationships, I am met with a polite disclaimer.

'Just so you're aware,' she tells me, 'I don't interview for works that will minimise the harms of sexual harassment and violence. I expect that you aren't planning to do so. Still,' she continues, 'I've been surprised in the past. There are a shocking number of women doing anti-violence work who make exceptions, especially for men they have loved.'

Wouldn't it be nice, I think, if all women were sieved, purified of the chokehold patriarchy has on us? If never did we think to joust one another or—smaller again—to look kindly upon men we have long loved, as they herald on about a batty ex-girlfriend or how so-and-so's sister refused to laugh at a stray, sexist joke that one time, a gag that failed to land, and how peeved it made them, how idiotic she was to think they actually meant it.

*

Blaine remembers how it felt to usher her small body through a concrete alleyway towards a dusty room beneath one of her university's theatres. It was familiar footslog to where Greg would be waiting, flicking aimlessly through printouts and fiddling about with leftover props. He'd pretend not to notice her at first as she leant gawkily against a nearby wall. In those moments, she envied how busy he managed to keep his hands, how many bulletins he had stored in his den, each demanding he sift through them. She watched as he dawdled over the battered skeletons of bygone theatre productions: painted columns, cruddy lanterns, anything to engage his limbs before the inevitable ensued. Small talk, and then big, fractured sex. It is only then that Blaine would know how to be, know just where to place her own hands—be it on the splintered apex of a rickety table, or the cold stone walls—as Greg scrambled about between the inside of her thighs, his pants slouched by his ankles. Not once did he remove his shoes.

Afterwards, she'd walk briskly back towards her office. Lori, a fellow PhD student and a close friend of Blaine's, would often be seated at their shared desk. Blaine would tug a nearby chair out from beneath its table, and smile. But on those days, the days when she'd emerge from the poky hole beneath the theatre, hatched and raw, she appeared to Lori changed, different. Sometimes, of an afternoon, the two women would lie together on the quadrangle atop the green turf and talk. They were both far from home, stuffing their mouths stupid with the riot that comes with city living: dating, cocktails, not having to recite an idle hymn or Sunday prayer from memory. Sometimes they wouldn't talk at all. Instead, they'd just bask together in the hushed intervals of relentless study. Here, on the sunny stretch of grass, is where Blaine first told Lori about Greg, insisting she not tell a soul.

It confused Lori at first, to imagine Blaine that way: glossed in the old married man's sweat. There were others, women both she and Blaine knew, in similar predicaments. Grace, for example, whose bra straps peeked out from the soft earth of her shoulders in class. Her supervisor, an esteemed scholar of English Renaissance literature nearly twice her age, readily put her forward for scholarships and funding opportunities, given the two shared a bed at least three nights a week. Blaine did not swan around campus, lithe and eager. She did not take. She was erudite, cleverer even than Lori. It's not as if Blaine ever needed Greg, in the way one may assume a student who peels her body from that of her professor's every so often might.

In the lead-up to Blaine's mid-candidature review, she spent a lot of nights chewing gum at her desk, plugging away at her thesis. Lori too. But one afternoon, Blaine appeared in their shared office, pacing. Lori watched as Blaine's breath crashed against itself. She looked squarely at Lori and told her that Greg had been asked to act as her external reader. He was to write a report for Blaine's mid-candidature review, and the jig may as well be up. Lori did her best to quell it, but her body was aglitter with resentment as Blaine sat before her, her head in her hands.

Here is where one may imagine a flashy ending for Blaine. A stellar report. Greg's love spilling out and onto her academic milestone. Him, a cradle—compact and sound—rocking her in his arms, as accolades, completion dates and career opportunities teeter above the two of them, arranged into a classroom mobile. This was what Lori saw, at least. She could almost hear the tinny sound of unwarranted success leaking out from its plastic. As she nursed a hangover that afternoon, this is what she saw, making her hate Blaine a little.

When I tell my own family about the book that I am writing, they too lean on this tired assumption: that surely these relationships are procured by students eager only to seek preferential treatment. Women—who aren't even that *young*, my mother reminds me—who know how to cheat and suck and lick their way to the top. But during the review, as Blaine does her best to save face, and as her supervisors wax lyrical about her obvious victories, about how well-steered she is, how well she's doing, Greg begins. He looks at her with the vapid expression of a man who hasn't felt the warmth of her insides, who perhaps never even cared to. Then, he begins.

Blaine recalls how readily he made tatters out of her work that day. How he minced her thesis to bits. How, afterwards, when everybody closed their laptops and headed to lunch, she felt like a shadow of herself, all grey and loose and sad. How, she tells me, if she were to cry afterwards—or, God forbid, during—it would seem suspicious. But she wanted nothing more than to do just that. To sob. To pick furiously at some loose grout she noticed by accident, a hole between the bricks on the classroom wall behind him, halfway through his cruel spiel. To peel the clay from its orderly arrangement, and to escape.

As she packs up her things, alone now in the classroom where the assault took place, a new rage makes itself known to her. That selfish prick, she thinks. He *used* her! He had accepted the role as her external reader only to divert attention from the two of them, to appear trusting, professional, in front of his colleagues. It's not as if he awoke that morning and thought only of Blaine: her future, her study, what a review such as this means for her PhD. It has been months since the two had interlocked fingers. And now, here he is again, an on-paper stain.

*

In another city, Elsie entertains a fantasy she discloses only to me. It is not like the other fantasies she has, ones that involve galleries with high ceilings, awash with attendees, lining up to gaze upon her paintings. Or the fantasy that pulls her out of her sleep sometimes, unbearably so. In it, her father is old, which means he isn't dead. But this fantasy is different again, plucked from an angry impulse to be understood. She imagines what it would feel like to tell her tutor's girlfriend, Amelia—a tutor herself, who also taught Elsie—about how she has long memorised the hollow notes of bourbon on his tongue. How he used it on her, his student, time and time again. How, as awful as it is to now admit, she had never been touched like that, held in such a way. She was barely twenty-six. Harrison, however, was in his forties. 'I think if I'm angry at anyone,' she tells me, 'I'm angry at the female tutors. If this is happening to me and girls around me, they experienced the same or worse. How can they not know?'

When the #MeToo movement began, Amanda Petrusich wrote for *The New Yorker* that 'much has been made of a so-called generational divide in the way younger and older women have metabolised its lessons'. I recently visited my grandmother, who is made crooked at the waist after years of injuries and neglect, and who requires a near-constant walking frame to assist her small, frail body. She slowly, and painfully, pulled a straw from a dusty plastic packet from beneath her sink and handed it to me. 'Here.' And there it was: a hollow orange tube to accompany the can of soda I had found in the top drawer of her fridge. My grandfather sat unrushed at the dining table as she staggered about him, tending to his needs. He is still agile, still able. But she is his wife.

'Does it make me a hypocrite?' I ask Georgie, a man I am seeing who has spent much of the week in Melbourne visiting me, as the two of us drive back towards the city from my grandmother's house. Before long, we are far from the sprawling countryside, the decrepit town where she lays her head. I find it difficult to square the nature of my work with the nature of my grandmother's reality: a woman who sometimes quakes at the sight of her husband. Who has felt the architecture of his pink cruel fists. There, in that ruinous house, is where she will stay. It is all she knows.

While writing this, I attend my friend Joni's hen's party just south of the city. It is here that I meet her Aunt Filia, a staunch, older woman with pearly soft hair and a worldly expression. I notice quickly in her a mosaic of experiences, and come to learn she used to be a palliative care physician, as well as one of two women at the University of Melbourne to have completed her medicine degree way back when. As a student, she lived at Trinity College, the oldest residential college at the university. Joni speaks fondly of how, in old photographs, Filia can be seen in a trim lab coat, her hair blow-waved up and out like a bookish Dolly Parton. I am not surprised to hear of her unmistakeable presence, her assertiveness. 'What do you do?' Filia asks, curious. I tell her about this book, and she raises both eyebrows knowingly. 'It's a real issue, this one,' she admits, with obvious terseness. 'In my case, it was. And, let me just tell you, it's always about power.' As the rest of the attendees begin to gather around a handful of dishes, she leans towards me and whispers, before skirting away, 'It's always the ones with the big bellies and the little pee-pees.' If she wasn't so earnest, I almost could've squawked right then and there, taken aback by her brazenness. She describes to me a cartoonish villain, of great and obvious superiority, but does so straight-faced. Gruff, almost. I think about it for hours afterwards, and on my drive home I wallow in her description of her assailant. I notice my chest tighten, as if suddenly claustrophobic. I imagine, through some dusty sepia lens, the former days of sexual misconduct on campuses around the country, how routine it all must've been then, how candid.

Each evening, I sift through Helen Garner's *The First Stone,* curious. How puritanical she may find my take on this matter, how quick to condemn. I'd be lying if I said I don't find her book at least a little compelling. I appreciate how she writes to the intergenerational tensions between women. In it, she argues that a young woman's response to a wayward pinch or a cheeky remark has become hasty and priggish. That it is disloyal to the big woes feminism ought to care about, if it cares at all. This, I hate. Perhaps that's why I find Filia's remarks a humbling but welcome surprise.

I wrongly assumed older, academic women akin to Garner would imagine I am making a huge fuss over not much. That I am policing the eros and all of its mystique and shimmer with dogged scorn.

*

Unlike her tutor, Harrison, Elsie knows not to entertain her fantasies. It would be cruel to arrive at his doorstep, dressed in funeral garb, and demand answers. How demoralising, to interrupt a man as he prepares dinner for his partner by demanding he declare his misgivings to you. All the while, knowing full well that *you*, in all of your arresting, warm flesh, happen to be just that: a misgiving.

Instead, two years after the fact and plagued by the dust of an unsettled relationship, she emails him. It feels almost voltaic to do so: to draft an invitation-to-meet and have it sound like an alarm at the top of his inbox. He doesn't respond for a day, and she is almost sorry. But then a day turns into a week. A week bleeds into two. After the end of the second week, his silence swells. By the third, it manages to develop its own sickening pulse, a thing Elsie is now forced to nurse. She stops being able to bear it, so she rummages through their email chain and rediscovers his phone number.

While in a relationship with Harrison, the two had discussed the concept of grooming at length. They had, while wrapped in each other's bodies, decided that this wasn't that. The wooden walls around them creaked a little as they rehearsed their pledge in the dead of night: that wrongness did not live here. Harrison was dogged in his convictions. Wrongness, he decided, is forever unable to remove the ghastly mask it wears. So, if it were to reside here, they surely would've spotted it by now. Where was it when he lay, gleeful and doting with her? Why was it that she couldn't feel its furore—or, at the very least, the gruff of its stubble—as they fell asleep together all those times? 'Don't worry,' he insisted on many occasions. 'We are alone.'

Perhaps this is why she felt compelled to reach out to him after all these years. To tell him that time had wiped clear the cobwebs, and—in doing so—had revealed a wrongness. In this small gesture lived an eagerness to entrust him with an unexacting task. Time had lifted the loose, flat sheet from the overhang of her bed and uncovered a rotten thing beneath the frame, peering up at her. All she wanted to know was if he saw it too.

*

I notice, throughout my research, a frustrating observation. When processing relationships such as these—ones that are littered with putative power imbalances—women look to other women for an easily delineated map, a chart for how best to make sense of this mess. Here, they remain endlessly disappointed. Helen Garner carved enemies out of her subjects, two young women who reported an instance of sexual harassment, because she felt their reaction unfounded. Lori became chary of Blaine, sure—for a small moment—that Blaine was pulling the wool over her assessor's eyes in allowing Greg a spot on her assessment panel. Blaine and Lori both looked on at another female student, dismayed. A student who seemed to take gusto in her sexual influence over a doddery, venerable man with opportunities to hand out to his nimble flame. Elsie vibrates with resentment at the thought of how senior women in her department let men like Harrison keep up their charade. The researcher from Michigan remained wary as to whether or not I myself might have once loved my professor, and felt it necessary to pair her email with a polite but vigilant disclaimer. Rose looked towards other young women throughout her relationship with Samuel as if they too had been conscripted, and harboured a neat grudge because of it. The suspicion of women—from women—reverberates on repeat, again and again, while men frolic about in the playground of their desires, never far from it all.

I wonder, as I return to this observation, if we expect little of men when we notice them snared in the grips of their wants. Do we, at best, pity them, and at worst, rid them of any semblance of accountability? Where does this leave us as we scrounge about for answers?

3

I AM SEATED IN the courtyard of a bar in Brunswick, awaiting the arrival of a retired academic. He had admitted to me over message that he had been with two former students: one a kiss, the other a three-month fling. Surprisingly, he wasn't the only older male scholar I had been chatting with. There were a small, devoted handful. One man, older than my father, would wait until well past midnight to message me. We would engage in strange, heady banter for many hours. In the rousing swell of his voice memos, I'd find myself forgetting about the task at hand, eager only to glean the few-and-far-betweens of his life. There was nothing parochial in our exchanges, and before long I felt a part of his daily routine. Here, in our message threads, the little whims of his day-to-day life were hashed out in striking detail. I became aware of many truths: his foiled past relationships; how his small dog would traverse about the house, only to leave a trail of fur on every seat. I learned about his brief dalliance with bondage and even—for whatever reason—his height and weight, as well as a considered description of his frame. I know, because he told me, that he had received a black belt in martial arts. After I emailed him a portion of my manuscript, he stopped responding. It was as if, by reminding him of my undertaking, I had pierced through the soft pink fog of our secret bond. He claimed, as early as our first conversation, to have never slept with a student, compelled only to reach out to me because it was a topic he found intriguing. I may have even believed him. But now, I am less sure.

Eventually, Elliott walks into the courtyard. He is tall with a sharp jawline, and I stand to shake his hand. 'I didn't know what you looked like,' he reveals, almost sniggering. I find it a strange thing to say, given he must have known. Our interactions had only ever taken place over Instagram, where many photos of each of us resides, and so I knew exactly what sort of man to expect. He had a distinctive, hollowed-out expression, his oily, dark hair carefully parted. He slotted into the booth next to me, arms splayed outwards, as if in a bid to frame himself. Before long, I threw a handful of questions his way, some lewd and unforgiving, and—after three pints—the air around us had become dank and curious. I felt, for a moment, that if I were so inclined, I could close my notepad, tug a little at the loose seams of our quasi-professionalism, and place a warm hand on his thigh, and it would be as if I'd finally gone and done it, had scratched that deep itch of his, that want. Much like the first student, all those years ago, who had insisted he join her and a few of her friends for a drink after their last class of the semester. He didn't tell me her name, just that the summer dresses she wore made a flare out of her. He remembers the fabric, the printed florals, the unwholesomeness of it all. At a grimy club that night, her body—all sleek and promising—caved in to his, and the two kissed while her friends giggled in a nearby corner, enthralled. Yes, he felt old, he tells me. 'But fuck, it felt good.'

I am conscious, as I traverse into the desires of male professors, of my own past. Does it cloud my research? I notice how the ghost of me finds herself comfortably nestled into the booth of some bar, of how she yearns a little to impress these older, more perspicacious men. It's not necessarily that I set out to ensnare them or even to relish their company. I just, with tactful patience, follow their lead. I make myself a zealous witness to their wants, to how it feels—once more—to be chosen by them. This is where I hope to identify the conjugations of a certain language, to feel its cadence. If I feel it is only uttered in the early hours of the morning, or in the absence of inhibition, it is here I will go to find it. In all of the places I'm not meant to look.

How obvious the feeling is of being desired. How quick to spot but equally difficult to describe. This is why, when Cara tells me that Ivan wanted her, despite having never reached for the small of her back, I believe her. 'I just knew,' she says and sighs, and I am reminded of Elliott's searching eyes, and how—when the bartender called last drinks come midnight—I knew it was up to me, and only me, to call it.

*

Cara has soft, perfect cheeks and heart-shaped lips. She is never bored. If you ask her how she is, she will take a breath before answering, as if beholden. This is because the gesture itself—of expressing interest in another person—excites her. She can hold a conversation of equal depth with whomever she chooses, be it a roadside trucker, an artist, or even just a child who has strayed from his mother's side at a buzzy food market. When she looks at you, it's as if nobody has ever looked at you as keenly as this before, and somehow she knows this but can't remember how she does, so she holds your gaze a moment longer, just to see.

Cara is the kind of woman men slump at the feet of, hopeful for just a lone, small kiss. For anything, really. 'Just one, please! And then I'll leave you alone,' I imagine them pleading. She is lucky. Endowed with a beauty as fine-textured and timeless as they come. But Cara is less impressed by beauty than those around her. It is too easy, too plain. 'I'm often attracted to people I find a bit gross, if anything. People that surprise me,' she tells me. I think, perhaps, that this is how it all began. With Cara, at twenty-six years old, watching her teacher cloak his pale neck with a moth-eaten scarf. A man rendered cartoonishly dorky. She wasn't supposed to want him, and so she did. But she insists that it started long before that.

Cara dresses a handful of dark wooden tables with paper lining. By the end of the night, they will be stained with bolognaise and the occasional confession, marked in red pencil by a mischievous child who, before wishing her grandmother a happy birthday, devours a pint of soda. She's eighteen and waiting tables at La Salvia. There are dusty jars filled with olives and brine, and sometimes, on a Saturday night, Cara's parents will come to her workplace, insisting it's for the mushroom risotto and some arancini balls. Really, they just want to see her. 'Here she comes,' her mother will say, and her father will wink at her as she approaches them, smiling, ready to take down their order as if she doesn't know it off by heart already. Cara is paid in cash and finds it endearing how dated the establishment is, with its fake flower arrangements and trite Italian playlist, courtesy of a dishy on his gap year who hogs the aux cord. On a quiet shift, she will take her time dusting the plastic roses. Sometimes, she will chat to Oz, La Salvia's chef, who takes a quick liking to her. He is churlish and sweaty, and the slit in his eyebrow always looks a little overgrown, despite never seeming to fill out all the way. If he catches her texting somebody, he will playfully reprimand her. 'Your boyfriend can wait,' he hawks, as if right from the beginning he had a habit of imagining her held.

Most weekends, Cara will walk home after work. She likes the small trek, the way the crisp air feels on her cheeks, how it tries its best to hose the garlic off of her. She tells Oz this, declining his insistent offer of a ride. Her evening strolls are when she makes a quilt out of her week's dilemmas, like what to say to Mr Jackson the next time he scolds her for wearing red lipstick to homeroom, or whether or not to wear a strapless dress to the formal. The suburbs at night are remarkably quiet, and being a teenager is not. You are always running towards, or away, from something. This, Oz doesn't understand. He is thirty-two and stagnant. He batters cauliflower five days a week and makes faces when his mother asks him, for a third time, to fold his washing, or tells him that the floor is no place for clean boxers. So he closes his door and yells at her for peering inside, for finding mess where she shouldn't be looking for it. He tells Cara this eventually, once she agrees to cop a lift home. That he cannot wait to move out. That his ex-girlfriend is a bitch, and that his mother is a bored, bonkers housewife with nothing better to do. Cara winces but listens all the same.

The first time he kisses her, it is urgent and ample. It comes after a weighted silence, as the two are stationary, parked fifty-odd metres from her family home. His red Honda Civic is where they spend their Saturday nights, long after the restaurant has closed, ruminating on one another's lives, their wants. He kisses her hard, and at first she almost recoils, as he tastes exactly as she imagined he would, all stale and with a mouth like an arsenal. Later she wonders whether she would've smelt danger on his breath if he hadn't told her about his big sorrows or made her laugh all those times. But only then does she think this, only later. Only once she notices the cruel outline of his body leering from outside her window in the dark one night, or learns to screen the eighty missed calls that appear on her phone from various numbers. Only once he insists that he will kill himself if ever she is to leave him.

'This, I think, is when I paired repulsion with desire,' she tells me. Because despite it all, the sex they eventually had on the leather seats of his hatchback was feverish, heroic. He'd pull at the soft silk of her hair, and wrench at her underwear, and her body would sing out for it, as loudly and as long as it could. This man, with his obnoxious voice and tangy skin, was not the sort of man she was meant to want. He would saturate his neck with cheap, acidic cologne and roll up the sleeves of his tight buttoned-up shirt before taking her out for breakfast, and she'd squirm. A girl from school, after noticing the two holding hands on a residential street, would later call him old and creepy. But in the warm bunker of his car, she found something rich and fulsome. There it was, in all of the places she wasn't meant to look. Now she knew how.

*

The first time she clocks a man's desire for her, Rose is eight years old. Her father places his big, safe hands on the small of her shoulders and introduces her to an associate of his:

David, a crusty older gentleman with a chummy smile and a round, hard belly, who playfully smacks her father on the back whenever he makes an off-beat joke. He is a bullish sort, and Rose's father—a man of barely twenty-seven—dotes on him because of it. Her parents are hosting a good old-fashioned barbecue, and David has arrived alone. Shyly, Rose stands before him. Taking his time, he leans down and, once eye-to-eye with the child, sighs. 'Thank you for joining us, Little Miss Universe. Aren't you something?' he offers, and she blushes.

She is eleven the first time a boy kisses her. At the tumbledown car yard his grandparents live in, protected by two idle Great Danes in cold metal chains, she hides out in his dusty room and watches him play PlayStation. They are family friends, and she is sleeping over. His father runs a tattoo parlour in town, and his mother—who hates his father—has veiny, cold hands and teaches Rose what 'see-you-next-Tuesday' means. While his grandmother smokes cigarettes and flicks through a tired Stephen King novel as she melts into the splintered leathery armchair in the living room, the two children watch *The Jerry Springer Show* together and alone in his bedroom, in terrible silence. 'She's hot,' he'd say whenever a girl appeared on the screen. Rose would nod impartially. 'I guess,' she'd say. An advertisement for Philadelphia Sweet Chilli Pourover begins to play between the commotion, and when the man in the commercial tips the plastic tub upside down, only to surrender the sauce from its canister, the boy quickly reaches for Rose's lips. He plants a wet, curt kiss on her, and laughs nervously afterwards. She doesn't wipe her mouth, but wants to.

By the time she meets Samuel, she is nineteen. She remembers it fondly: the heat of his smile that first day, how delightful it was to hear him speak. The deep vowel of her name, so sharp and considered, when announced during roll call. 'Rose?' he summoned, and for twelve weeks he continued to, as if plucking the sequence of letters that made up her name from some cosmic ether. It's then that he'd look up from his sheet of paper, pen in hand, to find her beaming back at him. By nineteen she was familiar with the febrility of men, the quicksand force of their wants. Despite having only fallen in love one-and-a-half times, Rose had been fumbled with at many junctures, had endured male desire at its absolute zenith, and, of course, at its laziest. She doesn't want him to know this. Instead, she wants to appear to him unruffled, untouched. With him, she thinks, she can leave it all behind. Start anew. So can he, she reasons. After all, he had made a small mention to the class one afternoon, midway through semester, about the break-up he had just weathered. Upon hearing this, another female student had let out a weaselly, ailing noise. 'Aww,' she purred, cocking her head as if to place it on some imaginary shoulder. Rose hates this other student's silky gesture, feels it could chip away at the lining of Rose's own conquest. For Samuel, she does not want to compete.

When romance blossoms in a classroom, ancillary characters—other female students, for example—become wedged, like knots, in the fabric of its story. Here, Rose straddles two discordant truths: she is both her tutor's admirer and his pupil. She can't discern the difference, which makes everything, and everybody, a threat. If one of Samuel's students, for example, spends her Friday evening cooped up in a university library, eager to refine the third draft of her philosophy assignment, Rose decides instead that she is weaving together an unbidden love letter. That hiding in its passages is a rambling secret, an invitation.

Rose is competent. She knows that she's good, and so does he. Every high distinction he gives her is proof. Later, well into their relationship, she will gloat about it, declaring herself his most astute student over the years. He will correct her when she does, reminding her that Damon—an undergraduate who wore moccasins and washed the topsoil off carrots during his volunteer shifts at Wholefoods, the student-run co-op at university—received better grades. 'Yeah,' she'd start. 'But it's not as if you fucked Damon.'

'No, it's not,' I interrupt, when she recalls this to me. 'But how do you feel about a comment such as this now, given he did eventually sleep with other students?'

I find it uncomfortable to ask a woman how she felt the first time she made sense of herself as a man's prototype. I feel like a burden in doing so. But I'm curious: where did Rose end and his new girlfriend begin?

She pauses a moment, and then—with a scant smile—introduces me to Samuel's latest, as if she, the third student, is nothing more than the thumbnail of a character, the apogee of Rose's own novel. She is described first in animal parts: all nimble and pretty, with a blonde pixie cut, pointed limbs and brimful eyes. Sienna. For reasons I am yet to fully understand, this is important. If she were run-of-the-mill, or even just fine-looking, what would be the use?

In the early days, Rose trusts him. Samuel treks through his routine unimpeachably. She wakes each morning and hears him. Beneath the hot stream of water, he lets his right hand wander, and seemingly makes do with some nameless, faceless thought, the smutty outline of some stock image gyrating a little behind his eyes. Sometimes she catches him on purpose, pulling back the shower curtain and laughing as he lets go of himself, shocked. He packs his briefcase, adjusts his jeans and heads into class. Sometimes he'd walk with a handful of his students through the quadrangle afterwards, insisting he had seen them around before, perhaps in some dive bar or waiting for a coffee in line at one of his usual haunts. This, Rose thinks, was his way of coaxing female students out of the classroom. 'Look at us, with our big, stirring lives, our similar worlds. We could've met elsewhere, you see.'

It takes Rose nearly five years to arrive here with me. A lot can happen in that time. Her and Samuel, after all, had been together for a long time. There had been many a milestone. Like how her and Samuel's cat has been made limp from a seizure a handful of years ago. How a man, older and greater than him, squeezed the soft of her thigh one evening, which she did not stop. All it takes is a call from Ellen, who bears for her a third recruit, to set the wheels of her new timeline in motion. She types the woman's name—*Sienna*—into Instagram's search bar and considers at first messaging her but hates imagining a lonely request hanging between the two of them. Can't stomach the stench of her own life as it hovers in the slimy hush of yesterday and each long day before then. After all, how do you explain away the ghost of yourself, who chose to stay with a man who made a mockery out of you?

Rose is silent, furious. She hates him for this. How tremendously wrong it feels, how shameful. With her, he had been so considered, so good. She had made the first move two years prior, long after semester had ended. Had sent him a coy message and had hoped for the best. Before long, the two were holding hands and prancing through Carlton together, full-hearted and buzzy. It was almost that simple. But here, by sleeping with another student, he was shameless. Had led her out from the brown architectural pasture where he'd found her and made an obvious mess of his wants. Rose can't shake the image of her from her mind. She wonders if she, too, had been seated on the bus the morning after the first time and had messaged a friend of hers to tell her that, 'Yes. I slept with my professor.'

The thing is, Rose couldn't ever imagine herself expunged from him. Until, of course, the third arrived, bringing with her the smooth recurrence of his own weather patterns, the reliability of a season.

4

Somewhere, as I write this, a man is speaking ill of his beloved. He is describing her as some vile weed, all bitter at the stem and prickly to touch. Perhaps she is his wife, and he is bored. She sighs every time she wipes the countertop and no longer appears to him fawn-like and soft. When she enters their bedroom after a shower and peels a bra from her drawer, he holds his breath, but not like he used to. It isn't caught and heady, twitching like a tendon after a big beast of a run. It is trapped, and so is he, so elsewhere he looks.

If he's Greg, it's easy enough. He snakes about his classroom and recites the words of long-dead scholars, adding his own inflections. There are students he notices: women who browse through their handwritten notes as he performs, who underline a note if he raises his voice a little. Charlotte, his wife, is discerning and far less impressed. If ever his female students email him, he is jocular in response, pairing his replies with typed-out smiley faces. Blaine, however, no longer needs to resort to such regulatory channels. Instead, they text.

Greg doesn't necessarily hide Charlotte from Blaine, but his marriage is hardly brought to the surface. If she cares to, Blaine must trace the shape of his wife's tracks herself, must scour alone, like a browsing animal, for her predator's imprints, for how they form in the path before her. She learns, courtesy of Facebook, that Charlotte is a nurse manager. She is well-dressed and stern behind the eyes, and Blaine is told that she, like Greg, is privy to a stranger's kiss. 'No,' she tells herself at various intervals. 'This is not an affair. I am not having an affair.' An affair would screech in the night, would wake her from her sleep with an off-key sort of howl. It would make a lonely, crying mess out of Greg as he crouches naked at the base of his bed, his head in his hands, insisting that he can't stand it any longer, that the guilt has corroded him just enough. Instead, Charlotte is an elusive housemate with marital rites. She is never, and always, there.

One evening, early into their relationship, Greg invites Blaine to attend an improv night he is hosting. Under stale blue lights, he escorts his audience into laughter. He is something of a triumph on stage, and in the second row from the front, Blaine sits, adjusting her skirt, and smiles keenly at him. Here, in this community hall, she does as she has long done: she marvels at his repertoire. As she waits for him to notice her, to gift her a small nod or a gentle smirk between the on-stage dialogue, she looks around and takes in the small crowd. It is then that she spots Charlotte, seated a few rows behind her, tucking a piece of her young son's hair behind his ear. Frozen, Blaine counts the dark red stripes of his wife's blouse and feels a rattle, a sickening clatter, between her ribs. Charlotte's legs are crossed, and so Blaine is able to notice her laced brown shoes. She has seen them before, placed neatly in the corner of Greg's bedroom. 'Where is she?' Blaine had asked then between breaths. 'Charlotte has her own fun, Blaine,' Greg insisted, before peeling the trousers from her hips.

While writing this book, I am asked to speak at a conference on reproductive justice in Brisbane. I arrive, and the balmy air sits atop my skin, laced with the salty promise that warmth brings. Conscious that I am in Blaine's city, that the two of us are mere kilometres apart, I invite her to meet me for dinner. Later that evening, she finds me on the steps of a small, paved street and grins, dressed in the amber light of a nearby restaurant. How easy it would be, I imagine then, to fall in love with her. There's an elegance to how she carries herself, and a shyness too. She is different from Rose, in that she does not cry out for some wretched opportunity to get even. It is too guilty a pleasure. She does not care to bare her teeth, or raise her fists, or satiate some tremendous hunger. Instead, she is precise. If given the opportunity to peek beneath the net of some grubby want, she wouldn't take it. I have to ask myself, as I do with each of the women I have chosen to write on: why her? I think, perhaps, this is the same question that haunts the core of each of their tangled histories. 'Why me?' When the dust settles and the men return to their pay cheques and papers—and, in Greg's case, wives—the query remains unfurled. 'Why did he choose me?'

It is a little after midnight, and Georgie is deep in one of his edits when I badger him about it. He looks up from his laptop, and I ask him, 'Why do you think I chose these particular women?' After all, there were many applicants eager to offer up their unique mistranslations of love and loss. For the better half of a year, my private messages were lined with confessions from various women, earnest in their want to share their story. There was a student at Oxford whose professor boasted, on their first and only date, that a handful of men in the department would be swallowed up by jealousy knowing he was here, eating oysters with her. And the fine arts tutor who drew red circles around his student's breasts when she handed in a series of nude self-portraits. This study of mine was never about scandal or R-rated impropriety. It was only ever about power and desire. 'What did you see in them?' Georgie begins, curious. 'Or maybe you need to ask yourself this: did you see something in them that their professors didn't see, or something that they did?' I think what strikes me about these women is far more personal, far closer to the bone, than I originally realised. In all of their clinking truths lives an ache I know well. A searing desire to be seen, to be plucked out of the humdrum of what once was and noticed.

*

In 2023, and only once made raw, Elsie decides to call Harrison. It rings out. Her room becomes dizzyingly still. She makes her bed, places her phone on the duvet cover, and collects a nearby towel from its hanger. It is then that she stands, motionless, in the pit of a narrow shower. She does not want to re-enter the world. Neither does she care to keep standing, so she slumps onto the tiled floor instead. The soft of her body flattens on the ground, clogging the drain. Elsie notices how water—with no place to go—swells before it scatters. So she moves, and the stream gurgles loudly because of it, making up for lost time. Her hair is nearly dry, and her toast nearly cold, by the time he responds. 'What's going on? Are you able to explain it over text?' he asks. His words, to Elsie, are so brisk and cruel. 'I guess he just couldn't be bothered to meet in person,' she tells me.

Harrison, although perturbed, eventually agrees to see her. He suggests a pub, despite it being the middle of the day, a site between both of their homes. Elsie hates the idea. She's not sure she can stomach the weight of booze with him. The clink of a pint glass, the stench of malt. How blowsy and awful he'd get after three-too-many. She yearned, momentarily, for a previous time, the era of her young life in which he wasn't a total nuisance, a drunk. Back then, he'd tidy his desk at the front of their classroom before a session and let his good, honest eye for art do the talking. She'd listen, hardly distracted by his taste. By the mild waft of booze that shadowed him, the mist of lemony cologne on his collar. When she arrives at the Union Hotel that day, his beer is already half-sunk. He does not stand to hug her but bows his head slowly, gesturing towards the empty seat across from him.

Women will wait their whole lives for an apology. Elsie can no longer wait. She learned, as she watched her father's body being lowered into the wet soil a few years ago, that time is a ruthless beast. It is not the sort of thing one gambles.

Just last week, I combed through an old handbag for a pen. Every so often, I will discover a discarded purse in my wardrobe and enlist it for a handful of weeks. I find, scattered in its belly, a smattering of filters, the crinkled wrapper of a piece of chewed gum, a receipt for petrol. This time, while searching for a nylon tip, I unearth a handwritten letter. It is creased in fours. 'Fuck me,' I whisper to myself. Two years earlier, a man I once knew—the same one who I met in a poky university classroom in my late teens—penned it. He had been offered an esteemed job in another state and thought it best to jot down how much it pained him to leave. How he hoped we could remain friends, despite the distance. Here, while caught up in the firestorm of this book, I entertain setting it alight. How satisfying it would feel. Or even better, to hurl it here, into this manuscript. To watch as its edges become singed by the inferno I've laboured over, the same one that can be found in the basement of some of Australia's most prestigious institutions, if only one cares to look. If I could, I'd tightly squeeze the shoulders of my teenage self, shake her a little. Twice even, as I'm sure she wouldn't listen the first time. I, too, grew weary waiting for an apology from him. So I peeled open my laptop, cast a wide net and decided—instead—to write.

Elsie remembers how Harrison forgot to ask her how she was that day. Their conversation was starved of pleasantries. Every souvenir of their time together, every question she had—'Why did you continue to pursue a relationship with me after we slept together the first time? When I was still your student? Why this? Why that?'—he'd explain away, whistling together big words and pairing them with even bigger reasons. She hated his stupid homily, how a man could appear so fearful in her presence while delivering it. Elsie has always been slight. Frail, almost. She has soft cheeks and papery wrists. He, on the other hand, has grey stubble and the gristly pink skin of a man who has long sunk piss. It becomes obvious, after some time, that he didn't come here to apologise. She decides to leave, and as she wanders towards the nearest tram stop, each step becomes more biting, more leaden, than the last. Elsie notices a child on the street, who jerks her father's arm eagerly. A child similar in age to Harrison's son.

The next day, still furious, she calls him and utters, as if with a mouth full of acid, 'I need to know. When did you realise you were using me?'

'It took me a little while,' he says.

Three months into their relationship, the two had decided to come up with pseudonyms, so that—if ever they were to message or call one another—obscurity kept them protected. Elsie had settled on Robert after Robert Delaunay, a modernist artist the two greatly admired, who co-founded the Orphism movement with his wife and fellow artist, Sonia. Elsie would wait for Robert's calls, for Robert to consign readings, to purvey rich texts and—occasionally—to ask her what she felt like for lunch. Robert, who would scrub the day clean of its bullshit. If ever she were imprecise or lazy, Robert would redirect her, reminding her that she's cleverer than that. One evening, while seated together deciding on a documentary to watch, Elsie thought to message Harrison a photograph she'd taken of the two of them that day for safe-keeping. His phone buzzed on the couch next to her, and there a four-letter moniker appeared, a name trite and random: Jane. How silly she'd felt, assuming that when he became Robert, she'd naturally become Sonia, the renowned modernist herself. Robert's equal. But no, she was Jane. He had meant no harm, of course. It was just the first name he thought of.

Plain Jane, Jane Doe, just Jane. Here, on the corner of Sydney Road and Dawson Street, Elsie wondered if it was then that he realised. That, yes—he was using her. That this was all just fodder. That, when Sonia Delaunay said of Robert in 1911 that in him she 'had found a poet, a poet who wrote not with words but with colours', her husband never once questioned that she too knew how to make pigments sing.

'A while later,' he offers. I wonder if it was only once he began a relationship with Amelia that he realised he had, the year prior, used Elsie. Perhaps, in procuring a relationship with a woman his own age, he found himself spooked by Elsie's girlishness. There are few pilgrimages as clichéd as fucking your student who happens to be half your age. Had he betrayed himself by having sucked on the poison berries? Everybody knows where they tend to sprout, and his teeth and gums were stained now with their juice. He didn't want to have to explain himself to Amelia, an esteemed painter herself who, having also taught Elsie, would never have been able to take Harrison seriously again. Not after learning that he had clung to some useless want months before he had clung to her.

Given how my interest lies in power and desire, what does a hankering for young women—particularly a young woman who is also his student—tell me about Harrison and many a man like him? Is it how a desire such as this makes what is most salient, most attractive, about a woman her proximity to youthfulness? How it decides women are sexiest if most able to fit under the thumb of their jaded, middle-aged admirer? Am I too harsh in how I have long come to pigeonhole this desire, to poke fun at it from some other stoop?

When Harrison admits this, Elsie feels as if her heart is strung up. She is familiar with its yank, and each time it wrenches and wriggles, she thinks, 'Well. This is all just a bit unfair, isn't it?' Perhaps this is why, after reaching out to me in January, she disappears for a while. For six calm months, she barricades herself from any kind of knockback, careful to sniff out the slightest reminder of any inkling of Harrison's carelessness. She archives every carousel of photographs from her Instagram page and falls asleep on the grey sands of a beach in Puglia. She picks seeds from her teeth and attends exhibitions alone, where arcane structures in big, cold warehouses speak to her in hushed riddles. But eventually she returns. I receive a message from her, late one evening in July, while labouring over the stories of Blaine, Cara and Rose. 'Ciao, Madison,' she begins. 'I think I'm ready.'

*

Cara's legs dangle from a swing set at Darling Gardens while Ivan is seated on a bench nearby. He watches as she thrusts her feet into the ground and lurches her body into the air. They have spent the morning taking a slow walk, only to arrive at the playground after an hour of ambling through the city's fringe. At first, Cara doesn't know what to make of his quietude. Are her enquiries silly? She doesn't think so. Ivan will chew over each one with careful fidelity. Sometimes he will even counter her points with greater, more sophisticated ones. Before long, the stillness between them becomes expected, and Cara notices even now how, since Ivan, she tends to pause. Will ruminate a little longer in conversation, and only then will she open her mouth.

Speech is where the two affix to one another, how they touch. His vowels are syrupy. If she can compel his vocal tract to warble its big, smart claims, if it is the only place they are ever to meet, then so be it. Arousal can make for dumb, gooey remarks, even from the smartest people: like 'I want to suck on your tits', or 'Show us your big cock', or 'Tell me I'm a slut', or something equally as derivative. Cara considers dirty talk delicious. Yes, it is the junk food of intimacy, but with Ivan she can appease herself otherwise, can nibble on the haute cuisine of their conversations, the airs and graces of good, honest nourishment. I think dirty talk is funny, really: in any other context, to speak so bawdily about how horny you are, how your animal body throbs and leaks, is inappropriate. But so is spending your Saturday morning dawdling through a park with your professor. If ever Cara were to crack, to admit to having fantasised about having him, it would make for too much wrongness here. So the two carry on, unencumbered by each of their inscrutable desires.

One evening, Ivan suggests that the two get ice cream. She agrees, and they walk to an ice creamery in Fitzroy North. He orders the chocolate fudge, she the vanilla bean, and the two decide to perch up on a seat in the street and finish their dessert before it melts. As he licks at his serving, a little enthralled by the taste, Cara feels something analogous to pity. Here, he isn't some masterly scholar seated at his desk who fingers through one of the many books he has authored. He doesn't wait for her eyes to pop. Here, his silence is accounted for. It lives between each swallow. His teeth may even rattle a little, courtesy of the cold sweetness. To see him like this—made curious, childlike, by something as flimsy as hunger, or even just pleasure—is to see him changed. It is brief, this terrible glitch in the matrix of their relationship, but it is felt. 'You see, in moments like that, I really felt as if I had more power than him,' she tells me. 'I was young and pretty. There's control in that.'

On our first date, Georgie and I don't have sex. Instead, we talk for hours. I introduce him to the book I am writing, and I am almost skittish, made a little berserk by the burden of holding a million-and-one secrets. It is as if, in becoming comfortable in the colosseum of out-of-pocket behaviour, I have moved past any such laws of courtesy and discretion. I am hardly coy, even offering to play some of the audio messages I have received in my expedition so far. He and I are seated opposite one another, and each time the old man with the tinny voice makes a flirtatious remark through my phone speaker or breathes a little too hotly under the collar, I smile fixedly at Georgie, as if to say, 'Look! Creepy, right?'

I can tell Georgie is interested—both in me and the subject matter—and, before long, he brings to light a story of his own. It starts off modest, an account of a previous time that is both small-boned and probing, a little like him at twenty-two years old, the time in question. He doesn't seem sure how to place it. After all, Georgie has arrived to me fully fleshed: handsome, triumphant in his chosen field, secure. He is hardly malleable. He speaks of his past as if it written in braille, all raised and ribbed in the right areas, but fiddly all the same. In his retelling, he is a young and sure-as-hell promising director, and everybody in the company where he is stationed knows it. In fact, they are so confident in him that two of the producers take turns letting him drive their cars, while they, on their full licences, offer to log his 120 hours so he can sort out his P-plates. There is an older woman, Kenzie, a producer at a neighbouring production facility. She wears suits and goes to hen's parties and notices Georgie immediately. It is only later—after the two have had sex—that she admits to having taken creative licence, to having shaved a year or two off of her real age, so that their romance felt less precarious. Less precarious for whom? I wonder.

When it comes to power imbalances, age is one salient ingredient. But it is not the only one. It is, in a lot of ways, a factor that piggybacks other disparities of power. There are significantly more relationships between older men and younger women, for example, making age the loose braid of a two-fold power imbalance. Gender and heterosexism drenches the field upon which generational divides play. I've come to notice that Rose, unlike the others, is evasive when I ask her about the age gap between her and Samuel. After all, he was only a handful of years older than her. She resents the narrowness of this language. She wants to know if it matters, if a few extra years would make a lampoon out of him.

'Does it matter?'

Yes … and no. It is so bare, so dull, for her time with him to be made blunt because of it. What she wishes she could say is that at nineteen years old, she was an island. She was the only member of her family to have finished high school, let alone enrol in university. Is it more or less pitiful, then, that a tutor in his early twenties appeared to her as magnificent, as erudite, as he did? That, as he paraded about the classroom, the skew of his big, elegant words were made all the more exceptional, almost in virtue of him being young? Perhaps if he were a long-in-the-tooth sort of man who wore cufflinks and called her darling, she'd be less swayed. If the relationship had clobbered towards her in a dusty, horse-drawn carriage and hadn't seemed so easy, so unremarkably plain, she may have found herself spooked. But she wasn't spooked. She was sure, then—once the two had made plans to meet for dinner and drinks on a Tuesday evening all those years ago—that nobody seated at any adjacent table would, or could, look twice.

'You know … if the buck stopped with me, and he hadn't done it a third time, I wouldn't be here,' she insists. I believe her. This, I understand. Two weeks after finding out about Samuel's relationship with Sienna, she takes a long walk. After twenty minutes, the clouds above her darken, making for a menacing sky. A vicious, sideways downpour ensues, and she runs all the way back home atop the mess of asphalt. Her breath starts to heave. Then she is angry. In the hallway of her house, her clothes now hefty with the wetness of a storm she hadn't thought to predict, she screams. If only she'd checked the forecast, but of course she hadn't. She is twenty-eight years old and embarrassed. She cannot remember the last time she felt herself defeated by such an ugly, honest tantrum. There, on the floor of her hallway, her body heaves big tears. Only once it stops and she manages to calm herself down does she retrieve her phone from the damp back pocket of her jeans. She punches 'safer community unit' into her search bar. The hotline pasted in the centre of its page taunts her, dares her to call it. Her confession, framed with each soft, sad buzz of static. A woman answers, and Rose's voice arches into form, becomes a thing of tart professionalism. 'Yes, hello,' she begins. 'I'd like to report a historical instance of sexual misconduct.' This is how it happens, how it all takes shape. How, once made to rot, she forgets how not to stay rotten.

5

We each have our breaking points. For Rose, it was a third affair. With the knowledge of this student, Samuel's legacy in her life becomes its own mangled glowstick, something that—once snapped at the spine—makes for the most garish, dreadful light. Everything from here on becomes a fluorescent mess: every holiday they took, program they watched, joke they made. 'I guess what I'm saying is that once you see it, you can't unsee it,' she offers.

For Blaine, the blueprint of Greg's prophesy is less tangible. Instead, she is left with a small hunch. At first she almost refrains from looking into it. But Greg is less careful now, and so Blaine is able to steal an occasional glance at it from across the room. It scowls at her from the horribly familiar fork-in-the-road of their affair, of her having been his student. It, of course, being Jenna: a younger, newer prospect for Greg to yield to.

Blaine is thirty-five years old when she meets Jenna. Jenna, on the other hand, is twenty-five. She wears perfume that whistles in soft nectarine tones and, in the classroom Blaine now teaches in, is quick to raise her hand, to solicit discussion. They get along, in much the same way that Blaine gets along with all of her students, who each appear to her young, hopeful and a little frazzled. On Wednesday afternoons, Blaine arrives to class armed with two packets of sour worms, as she has noticed how quickly their attention wanes just before teatime. She has long been courteous like this, considered. Energy is energy, and they need all of the help they can get. She doesn't care that the other educators think it a little patronising, especially Greg, who is now assigned the role of associate professor. Despite working in the same department as her, he is a man Blaine manages to give a wide berth to if, and when, she can help it.

One afternoon, Jenna requests to speak to Blaine after class. She fiddles with a loose bracelet as it dangles from her left wrist, before asking Blaine if she wouldn't mind formally introducing her to Greg. After all, she is approaching an important juncture in her academic trajectory. She is close to needing a supervisor and, given her specific line of inquiry, he seems the most appropriate fit. Blaine feels flushed. The familiar heat of anxiety rises in her gullet. 'Is my discomfort so obvious?' she wonders, almost certain that two wayward figures—a small angel, and her fiendish friend—have materialised atop of her shoulders, rustling about near her ears. Jenna doesn't seem to notice, and Blaine interrupts the invisible dialogue of her chums with a big, friendly smile. 'It's just … I heard he had quite a lot to do with your thesis back when you were a student, so you obviously know him quite well, and I don't want to just … shoot him an email out of the blue, you know?' Jenna says.

As Blaine trudges back to her car afterwards, she amuses two possible outcomes. The first: that her wariness is unfounded, and that Greg ought to be trusted with the task. That perhaps what happened all those years ago was a haphazard sort of blip, buoyed by the laxness of a different time and perhaps even Blaine's own wrongdoings. In fact, Blaine may even be doing something worse if she refrains from offering Jenna a leg-up in the right direction. But this sense of wanting to shield Jenna, to protect her from the seared wants of a man as opportunistic and wheedled by sex as Greg, is blatant. Blaine was not sufficiently warned. History is not going to repeat itself on her watch, she thinks. Once behind the wheel, she lets the inanity of talkback radio wash over her, in a bid to soothe or distract from her worries. It is only once she is home and her cat mewls for tuna and something to drink that she lets her mind wander to that other awful place. Her cat finishes his dinner and proceeds to dip his paw curiously into the bowl, to test the water's depth. She is reminded of Greg, of their last night together. Was she something of a trial run then, with nice legs and soft arms? A student he could play naughty with in the shallows of some unspeakable, unknowable wrongness? How deep, she wondered, did his curiosity run?

If Blaine refuses to offer Jenna access to Greg, she fears needing to contextualise it. She would have to introduce Jenna to who she was then, all slight and nervous, her skirt hiked up and ruffled in all of the ways it shouldn't have been. She'd have to recite how Greg hoisted himself into her while the rest of her peers carried on through campus unencumbered. After all, things have changed. Blaine now attends trivia nights and falls asleep on the couch with Luke, her boyfriend, while the blare of some hit-and-miss war film hollers at the two of them from the television. She marks papers in her office and knows the names of the baristas that grind the beans of her morning coffee at the nearby cafe she frequents. She has smile lines and no longer thinks to count the grey strands of hair that crop up in recurrent stints. But she is still Blaine, still eager to see the best in people, and so one afternoon she cc's Greg into a chain of emails with Jenna, closes her laptop and waits. This is not an alliance she wants to form, particularly not with her twenty-five-year-old student. She is eager only to see Jenna progress into a scholar in her own right. When I ask her what eventually happened, she groans. 'Nothing good, I don't think. But you know that, and so do I.'

A week or two later, Blaine receives an out-of-the-blue message from Greg, who thanks her. Jenna, he boasts, has wonderful taste in music. A real eye for poetry. It is as if Blaine has gifted him something, peeled back the curtain of some retired want, and offered him a seat there. His message reeks of the kind you send a casual friend who recommended some new television drama for you to binge. Blaine had never thought to ask Jenna, in the year she had been her student, about what kind of playlists she curates while she drives, about which album she listens to only when she is alone. Blaine is incredulous. She describes how it feels to me in sweeping emphasis. 'I was immediately repulsed. Apart from the embarrassment I felt, there was also that anger.'

To bear the outrage of many women is to square up with one's own. I'd be lying if I said it wasn't starting to sting. In writing this, I find myself weakened, susceptible to anger. On one particular morning, I crack. I'm not sure what does it exactly. But when I wake, I find that my last search on Instagram is Harrison's username, and staring back at me is a photograph of him eating a chole kulche with Amelia outside the gates of some illustrious artist residency in Delhi. Before long, I am typing out a message to my once-upon-a-time tutor, a man who pervades a lot of my thinking long after the fact. 'Hi,' I write. 'I'd like to speak with you. I can't make sense of this still, and would appreciate clarity.' I hit send and immediately I regret it. The circumference of my investigation becomes a thing crammed and tight, closing in on itself. I don't want this book muddied with question marks. It is not some punctuated hangover. Not some wretched journal or a means of catharsis. But as I zigzag through the big lives of the women I've chosen, I notice how absent in their anecdotes is any kind of justice, any full-circle moments. *These men, these fucking men.* Their wrists don't throb with the soreness of a slap. Their jobs aren't jeopardised. Their wives don't leave. Their children imagine them good, honest people. They are solid, sturdy and empty all the same.

*

At the cafe where Rose and Ellen are meeting, Ellen is already seated. Samuel's new girlfriend's name is flung back and forth between them like a thing too hot to touch. *Sienna.* She is an idea to both Rose and Ellen, a last-minute conscription in Samuel's tournament and, for Rose, something of a voodoo doll, whose straw hair Samuel combs and whose wool body he may as well be placing tiny pins into, only if his hairline especially recedes or if a paper of his is rejected. Rose admits to having looked for her Facebook profile and holds her phone-screen up to Ellen to reveal it, like it's a portal into some conspiratorial place. A ticket out. She doesn't remember how it happens, almost pretends to not have noticed Ellen's wariness around it, but she chooses to message Sienna right then and there.

The message is long and damning. It feels good, and dangerous, to write. They don't know this then, but by the time his girlfriend receives it, her breasts will have just started to ache. She will be made tender from the rebel hormones of a pregnancy. She will have decided, after just a small handful of months, to give her all to this man. Naturally, she will never respond to the message. Instead, she will adopt a dog. Assemble a crib. Thank Samuel for taking out the trash, wishing—in the quiet moments—that there was more he could dispose of.

*

I have made a clean, marked decision to centre this book on consensual relationships. Otherwise, the abuse is too obvious. And yes, I have heard many terrible stories. Haven't we all? Like blowjobs procured in exchange for research assistant positions. This was the last terrible story. These assaults, they pile up in excess. There are the men we all tiptoe around, who hail from many different watering holes. These are the ones I am less curious about. The ones that make car wrecks out of women. And then there's Ivan, who never orchestrates any such collision.

How does one account for Ivan, who vacuums the dirt out of his second-hand bohemian rug before Cara arrives? Who retrieves a folded wooden chess set from beneath a blanket, peels it open, lays out a pillow and taps on it mindfully, insisting she sit and play him? Who never lays a hand on her? I sense, at the beginning of our correspondence, that even Cara isn't sure. Ivan, to Cara, is an anomaly. Different from other men. I sense also that I am trying to make him fit the only way I know how: by insisting his behaviour is inappropriate. Not crooked, perhaps, but surely a little bit unseemly, right? 'Right?' I insist aloud.

'I don't know if it is that simple,' Cara tells me. There is a deep irony in me wanting to press out this man's presumed kinks, in wanting to have them—or him—made consistent with the other professors. Cara resists this. She has every right to, but I'm searching instead for patterns. To have her fit. She points to a place in her mind's eye and smiles, and I stand in firm opposition, insisting that if she just looks a bit closer, she will find that it is decayed or broken or both. It must be. And yet, I am the same woman who resents Samuel for making a pattern out of Rose, stencilling her likeness onto everyone he touches. And I am the same woman who considers Greg a similar sort of brute, just older, who readily volunteers his deepest secrets and the occasional voice memo of a song he has written to one of many female students, each of whom get more juvenile with time.

'There is one thing,' Cara tells me. A minor betrayal. Once Cara had graduated, she had been offered an esteemed job at a climate change institute, working as an advisor. The organisation had, in the past, accepted grants from a handful of funding companies in a bid to stay afloat. Some bodies had been less progressive than others, sure. But Cara wasn't as concerned with the back end of the operation as she was its output, with the solutions it offered. Money is money, and money is power, and—as far as she was concerned—it had landed in clean hands, so it had the freedom now to become something of cultural value. One evening, she had received an out-of-the-blue email from Ivan, who had congratulated her on her recent appointment. There was another caveat. He hoped to invite her to join him for a robust discussion over Zoom. Their exchange would be recorded and streamed online to each of his students, and their conversation would tackle big, meaty themes: namely, how one navigates practising good ethics in the climate change industry if their salary is fundamentally curdled by unprincipled donors.

There was something harsh in his request. A small cruelty. Was he making an example out of her? Turning her into something of a hoo-ha in front of his class? Was he masquerading his invitation for dialogue as an opportunity to point a finger, to reveal to his students where best *not* to end up if—of course—they claim to have a soul? The man was mutinous, then and now. She knew this, and so did he.

He had made an obvious judgement in his gesture. She had taken a job that didn't align with his values. He had watched on, disappointed, as she suckled on the teat of some enemy. Ivan had even offered to pay her for her time out of his own pocket, which made her feel queasy, as if it were the evidence she never received that their relationship had, after all, been transactional. She refused his money but agreed to talk nonetheless. The exchange felt accusatory and cold, like he was a journalist on some forbidding chase for scandal and she his subject.

He had pre-recorded their chat, insisting he would eventually show it to his class. 'Which class?' I ask, and she pauses before telling me that she never found out. She doesn't remember how he introduced her in the recording, isn't even sure the video was used for educational purposes. This exchange was the last time they spoke for close to four years. By calling on her for comment, he had returned her squarely back into his classroom, had looked at her with those nippy, unfeeling eyes and had managed to make synthetic all their nights together. 'I no longer impressed him,' she sighs. 'It was all so impersonal.'

When Cara eventually tells me this, I sense a small shift in her. As if perhaps Ivan was crueller than she originally thought. I do not set out to interrupt the lives of these women, to recast their memories so as to show them that beneath them a prophecy of worms can be found wriggling. If Cara had been resolute, if she had decided then that Ivan was a rarity among the commoners and only ever that, this I would've accepted. Would've had to. Nonetheless, I take this chink as an opportunity to ask her if there were ever any other students. If, to her knowledge, she had unlikely allies. If ever, on one of the nights Ivan and the rest of his class drank at the Carlton Yacht Club for knock-offs, she had noticed him scoping out another. She says no, and I believe her. This she has over the others. There is no Cara-shaped habit lurking in the hamlet of his mind. Yes, because when she left, she stayed gone. This, for the others, is an enviable thing. To be a person resurrected is to be made dusty with a life since buried. Is to be made haunted. That is, of course, how the old allegory goes. That even Mary became bloody the third time her name was sung.

*

One winter, during her relationship with Greg, Blaine developed a fever. Her head throbbed with a pulse all torrid and heavy, and even the soft fuzz of her arms stung. She knew, as he had mentioned it, that Charlotte was interstate for work. Lori, her PhD officemate, was busy, so Blaine asked if Greg wouldn't mind caring for her that evening. She hated being sick. A head cold could send her body into a tizzy. It would bind its sickness to whatever else it could find, which was usually just more sickness: an additional ache, an agonising period, an anxious spell. He agreed, and she climbed into a cab, covering her mouth and nose.

Blaine liked the tidiness of Greg's home, of how everything had a place. He poured her a glass of lemonade and she sat on his couch, tempted to place her feet onto the coffee table. Envious, too, that there was space to do so. Her family home had made for less cooperative furniture. It was stacked instead to the nines with old dusty magazines, hard rubbish and clean, unfolded washing still in its basket. She had been loved by hoarders, by a family whose habits revealed themselves in small, demanding piles. Of Tupperware and birthday cards stacked in excess. Of shame that couldn't be kicked and shoved into a bottom drawer already full, but it's not as if they didn't try.

As she laid in his marital bed, unable to sleep, her mind started to wander. All clogged up with no place to go, while next to her some old wedded professor drooled onto his costly linen sheets. It was not where she hoped to find herself. Yes, she was an adult, but how nice it would've been to have called her parents instead. To have them wipe the sweat off of her brow with a fresh, new cloth and for her feet to touch the naked carpet of a bedroom made open. She played on her phone for a while, hoping the blue light wouldn't wake Greg. In the dead of night, she revisited an essay she had read some years ago about compulsive hoarding disorder. It reminded her that many such idiosyncrasies are established patterns of behaviour, habits long unchecked. She closed her eyes and became young again, screaming as her sister held up the bloated relic of a long-dead possum by the tail, a creature made obscene only once flattened beneath some box in her grandfather's garage. To have habits such as this is to have life spoiled, soured. Years later, when she scours through her Facebook Messenger thread with Greg to refresh her memory for me, searching for keywords, she will type in h-a-b-i-t. There, she will find it. He endeavours to tell her, early on in their dalliance, that he has never made dating former students a habit of his. That yes, there had been a few at previous appointments, but it wasn't some matter of course.

Blaine eventually fell asleep that night, clutching a wet tissue. She awoke only a few hours later to find Greg gone, having commenced his day. Once she made the bed, she wiped her nose once more and left. The walk home from Greg's abode was long but not difficult. Before approaching her street, she noticed a house nearby that looked a lot like her parents' homestead, and she stopped. It stood choked by brown vines and haphazard equipment: a rusty lawnmower, a tiny swing set laying on its side, a few dozen picture frames, some plastic tubs stacked and teeming. She heard a dog bark from its guardhouse but couldn't see the mutt from behind the stained, drawn curtains. To hoard is to have so much and so little. Is to endeavour to fix the absence of something with the presence of many small things. She considered for a moment what tawny old doll in some back cabinet she was to Greg, or would become. What parts of him had he attached to her, unable to throw out? Because the professor who whispers sweet nothings into his students' ears makes sweet nothings out of them.

She continued on. Thought, after all this, who will find her? Who will hold up her memory, all flattened and grubby? And who—upon seeing it, not as it was but as it is now—will scream?

6

When it came to writing this book, I was wary to venture into school territory. I found its wrongness so obvious. The relationships between teachers and students in this domain lacked the slipperiness of adulthood and agency. But still, I returned to some deep gnaw: is the presence of youth the only discernible badness here? I was curious, not necessarily to argue that the wrongs committed in high schools by teachers towards their pupils are comparable to adult relationships between university staff and their students. I was curious instead as to whether or not the desire some teachers have to sleep with or hold their students was able to be culturally tracked. If I could follow the inception of some maladaptive want.

I remember there being whispers at recess when I was a high-school student. Stories that balloon long after they're done, about particular teachers and their bad affinities. Like the one about Miss Hunt and some boy in the year above me at school, who had small, ruddy craters on his cheeks, courtesy of cystic acne. They had been caught attending the cinema one evening after school, holding hands. Quietly, she was asked to leave. His friends had patted him jauntily on the back upon finding out, considered him victorious. This, after all, is the value of taboo in the young mind of bullish boys. Taboo entices and goads an otherwise eager audience, too young and engrossed in the allure of sex to appropriately recognise its harms. It is all fantasy, until it isn't. The schoolyard is a place where we all first learn how best to surrender, to seek external approval.

And then there's our childhood homes, where each of us are loyal pilgrims. Our complex parents, whose ruptures embalm themselves in how and who we love. When Elsie's father finds out that he is terminally ill, his impulse is to run.

He makes a quick, foolhardy choice and books a one-way ticket to Italy. But cancer does not wait at the terminal gates. It treads on the heels of its subject and wields its way into the air alongside him. Elsie flies to him in a bid to bring him home for treatment. He is experiencing seizures, and they both know he is not fit to fly. That twenty-eight hours buoyed up in the still clouds is no place for a man as sick as he is. She makes the choice to swallow her tongue, to keep hushed the state of his ill health. As each minute passes in the cabin, she feels the altitude pinch her nerves, looking every so often at her father's still face beside her as he naps. A year and a bit later, she will commit to her tutor's want for secrecy, knowing that, while his life is not in her hands, his career may as well be. Here is a woman who knows that when it comes to love, there is more to fear than getting caught.

These women—Rose, Cara, Elsie and Blaine—are each placed on some varying stoop when it comes to the snares of being found out. For Rose, there is no need to hide. Samuel is not her tutor by the time the two start dating. She even goes so far as to change her major so as not to end up in his class again. She insists to me that she does this of her own accord.

In Rose's life, Samuel is documented, paraded and loved outwardly. His name accompanies hers on leases and plane tickets and wedding invitations. Their origin story is marked over, time and time again, with greater milestones. A pet or two. A family dinner. This, I think, is how she protests. She becomes something aged and insistent. 'I was never hidden, don't you dare do it now,' is her outcry. Here, after all these years, is not where she will find herself erased.

Cara has her own reasons to conceal Ivan. She is in a relationship with somebody else at the time and savours the reprieve of being wanted elsewhere, of being able to let her eyes scatter over books that aren't hers or her boyfriend's. She can visit this secret, fanciful land and given Ivan doesn't ever make a mouthful out of her, she can return home, undrunk and uneaten. The secret is hers and only hers. The nights are as fleeting as she is, silken and passing, and she likes that. He never sees her cry, for he is not her boyfriend and it is not his job, and she likes that too.

For Blaine, it is different again. Greg is married, and she knows this. Blaine is a secret two-fold: the other woman in his life, carrying with her a romance that transpired on university grounds. Usually she hates to imagine herself this way. But during one of Greg's comedy performances, while the two are together, something shifts in her. The attendees, including her sister who she has invited along, are seated on stage among the comedians. They are each performing skits around the spectators. 'It's all quite intimate,' she tells me. As Greg cavorts on every side of the audience, she clocks how quick he is to notice her. There is a glum courtship to it, the way he frolics like something feathered and horny, performing his secret mating dance. It is as if it is just the two of them, and she wonders whether, if she were to kick out her leg from its skirt and he were to trip on it, maybe, just today, he'd thank her. Would kiss her toes and bow his head to her small, pretty feet. Only today does she think, *Yes. I seduced this man. I am in charge.* She could prise his wife away from their homestead if she wished, burn through his imitation armour with one piercing stare. Here, he is her secret instead. For a moment, surrounded by the laughter of strangers, she feels a brief power. He is on stage, but so is she. She continues to watch the other comedians while Greg keeps his eyes squarely on her.

In one of her tutorials, and less than a fortnight after Elsie and Harrison first sleep together, she notices a terseness in him. She observes him as he leans over her research paper all hawk-eyed. His feedback seems blunt and cold, and she can't understand why. Elsie is surprised, but she reminds herself that she is here not as his lover but as his student. Teachers, like the rest of us, have bad days, and as pupils you aren't placed to ask what's wrong. This language is reserved for bedrooms, not classrooms. So she doesn't ask, and come the end of the tutorial, Harrison puts a question to her, a cheeky aside. He quietly requests to know if anybody has found out about the two of them. Had she let slip? Had she sealed some envelope and signed off with the outline of a kiss she insisted he knew the contours of? Had she bundled up the night they spent together and handed it in to God-knows-who? Offended, she leaves, noticing another student curled over his laptop in the corner of the room, terrified that he may have heard.

On the tram home that evening, she messages him, insisting that she will not let herself feel bad or wrong for what happened between them. He arrives at the doorstep of her sharehouse barely an hour later, apologetic. 'Not for a second do I think that what happened between us was wrong,' he asserts, and for two big hours he invites her into the fold to peer behind the closed awnings of his world and ask away. This man, who offers tales of depression and longing, insists that if she just narrow her eyes a little, she will find they have more in common than she thinks. He isn't wrong, exactly. Her history can attest to this. Caring for her sick father has set her apart from her peers. Not many her age have held a syringe filled with morphine up to their parent, delegated to dull his pain with a quiet, small push. Those were hard times, especially when the measurements had rubbed off on the nozzle and she wasn't sure if she was giving him 5 or 15 millilitres of opioids. That day, having reassured her of his devotion, Harrison left relieved. When I ask Elsie how it felt to make her offence known to Harrison that day, she attributes her spunk, her self-assurance, to a kind of girlish confidence. To the fuck-it attitude of a student made special, a student who can roll her eyes at her teacher and get away with it nonetheless. Only years later does it strike her that Harrison's rashness to apologise that day was not a bid to right some wrong but instead to keep Elsie at bay, to pacify her.

*

'Do I live how you imagined me to live?' Ivan writes to Cara in a short email. A scarce and beguiling question. It is sent two days after she visits his house for the first time. She had accepted his invitation after a walk one afternoon, back to his quaint Clifton Hill bungalow, where he lived with two other academics. She didn't imagine him a man with housemates. After watching him take his shoes off at the door, she follows suit. Then he leads her into his bedroom, only to traverse about his small comforts, to make himself at home among his things. He moves as if in slow motion. There are blankets, posters and many a book, itemised by colour. Linen shirts made creased, hanging from an open cabinet. And then there's Cara, who stands by his open window and flirts with the idea of catching his eye.

They have punctured new territory, and neither necessarily knows what to do with this. It makes murky and exciting the obvious strain between them, and Cara imagines these four walls having not seen much sex or even the quiet promise of it. He is sexless, after all. Otherworldly. She takes a seat on his mattress, and he gads about behind her, summoning a hardback book from one of his shelves. He doesn't need to ask her if she's read it, for he knows that she hasn't. This is when he begins, pausing with each sentence, as if he a man eternally at knowledge's whim. A man forever studying. His voice thaws through her like a clergyman reciting a canticle, and she is made almost holy. 'Keep going,' she thinks, if ever he arrives at some interlude, some obvious beat. Behind the window, the sun retreats into itself and then it is dark. Nighttime gnaws at the two of them, as if to say, 'Go on.' It would be too easy, she thinks, to give the night what it clamours for. Too par for the course. She cares not to be struck down by some brutish impulse, to be made a thing that moans. So she leaves.

'I imagined you to live here,' Cara eventually responds to his email, attaching a stock image of a library, filled to the brim with books. She tells the man what she knows he wants to hear. Makes obvious that he is but an idea to her, a fantasy. Later, after she shows me this exchange, I will think about it for days. *Why?* Because I can't imagine being possessed with Ivan's confidence, of thinking to ask somebody a question as whole as this. *Am I who you thought me to be? Tell me your ideas, tell me who I am to you.* I hide instead and hope to not be discovered. The first time Georgie and I kiss, I become short of breath, dizzy. This is because I haven't eaten a whole meal in days and tiny scabs have formed along the rim of my hairline, the hostile result of malnutrition from having anorexia. This, I do not want him to know. I do not want him to see the whites of my eyes, the wafer thin of my skin, or how tingly I become after days of being hollow. Cara will long avoid inviting Ivan to her house. She does not care to be something known. So she remains afloat—sans a home, or friends, or a partner, or any kind of anchor—and meets him every so often, on the floor of his bedroom, for a heady game of chess.

In much the same way I am interested in how fantasies are maintained, I also care to understand how they are destroyed. Rose is too, and she describes one of many small endings for her and Samuel. The first happens out of the blue. One evening, close to a year into their relationship, she attends an event in the city with a handful of mates. Max, a friend of a friend, is performing spoken-word poetry, and Rose watches on, transfixed. Afterwards, her small group satiate their hunger by devouring two-dozen cheap, oily dumplings, and Max invites along Syed, a tall and impressive filmmaker. He is charming and significantly older than Rose, and just two weeks earlier she and Samuel had attended a screening of his debut film. 'I loved your movie, by the way,' she offers. He smiles, taking a quick and obvious liking to her.

After dinner, they all end up at a bar in the city and, before long, the rest of the ensemble have peeled away, leaving just Rose and Syed. He is self-assured and leans in to kiss her while they are seated on some outdoor patio. Taken aback, she retreats. She is flattered nonetheless. If she were single she may have considered it, but she isn't, so offers him her cheek instead. 'If you let me take you home, I will fuck your brains out,' he slurs forcefully, even after she is emphatic about having a boyfriend. She tells him that she best walk home, but he stresses that it is late. That the streets are no place for young women to roam unchaperoned. He offers to book her an Uber and she accepts, reciting to him her home address, but once the car arrives, he climbs eagerly into the back with her, making a mess out of her neck as he heaves atop her, kissing it. At once, she is nervous. His place is the plugged-in destination, not hers. When the car eventually pulls up at his apartment complex, he slowly pares his body from the backseat as if expecting her to join, but she doesn't, closing the door behind him instead. It is then that she is still, lifeless. The driver, a little stumped, suggests she rebook an Uber. 'Do I need to get out?' she asks, sheepish. 'No, I will take you home.' In the nine minutes it takes to return to her apartment, she recedes into herself, all guilt and brew. She quietly rehearses how best to fill in the gaps, to make it make sense for Samuel, who is fast asleep by the time she barges in, crying. 'I'm sorry,' she yelps. 'I think something happened, and I'm sorry.'

Rose does not remember much of what happens next. But she recalls that in the slick nuisance of his hurt, Samuel offers her an ultimatum. Straight-faced, he attests that she had either cheated on him or been assaulted. It was one or the other, plain and simple, and up to her to decide. She refuses to choose, pulling her doona up and over her cheeks instead. She wants to disappear. She thinks back to a previous time when she was sixteen and had fallen asleep on a makeshift bed in the back room of some house party. A boy from a neighbouring school had noticed her there, had wormed his way into her sleeping bag. She had awoken to him eagerly pressing his body against hers. 'I'd rather not, sorry,' she whispered. But he had already rendered her mute, pulled gently instead at the neckline of her T-shirt as if it were a thin lasso, and placed his mouth on one of her nipples. Generously, she thought, perhaps he just hadn't heard what she'd said. Rather than repeating it, she laid motionless, her mind blank and glassy. His hands went searching, and in their pursuit, they found her. But she couldn't feel them, could only see his silhouette as it welded itself to hers. In the morning, she approached him, embarrassed. He had been seated on a couch in the sobering light of day. 'You cannot tell anybody about what happened,' she demanded. It takes her three years to realise the truth of this incident, but every so often in the early hours of shameful mornings, it creeps into her mind once more and professes to know something she doesn't. It insists that she must've wanted it. That her yearning for sex and its echoes were so undeniable even then, that to render herself a victim would make for a bogus claim.

Given it is now 7 am and the birds have begun their arpeggios, Samuel brews himself a coffee. Then he returns to their bed and takes a seat on its edge. 'You know, Rose,' he begins. He is gentle, considered. 'Every day, when I am in class, I can tell that there are students that want to fuck me.' She looks up at him, a little confounded. 'You can?' she asks. 'Yes. And every day I choose not to, because I love you. I'd appreciate that same courtesy.' She nods, considers herself disciplined, and it is over. But the words loop spectacularly, as if some kind of forewarning. Remember how entranced she was, how hellbent she'd been while his student? She hadn't pondered their inception for some time, and in fact hadn't needed to. There had been bills to pay and houseplants to water and, come March, a dog to walk. But hearing now that he had long assumed the desire of his students a mere part of his employment contract and, like some self-described saint, had dismissed their calls? This made a riddle out of her. What made her *yoo-hoo* for him so loud, so discernibly obvious all those years ago, that it cut through the masses of some drooling, all-wanting cohort of female students? Is it the same thing that compelled Syed to make a mess of her neck? It is her desire that long ought to be disciplined? A light goes out in her mind and never turns back on.

7

It is 2009, and Blaine is distrait. Her bones jut out from the elbows of her sleeves, and her eyes are cloudy. She has begun grinding her teeth in her sleep, so when she wakes, her jaw is stiff and locked, like a pit bull's. All the soft railings of her body tremble, as is the case when there is hardly any meat on the bones. She is heatless, made all the colder because of Wesley, her boyfriend. He is cruel and unrelenting and will pull the rug of their relationship out from beneath her, breaking up with her for the most trivial of reasons. Like the time she'd booked aisle seats for a concert the two had planned to attend, and he'd wanted different ones. 'I was always on eggshells,' she tells me. University is a place safe and untouched by Wesley, somewhere pure and speckless she can retreat into. Here, she breaks the silence of home, of her terrible relationship. Here, she feels the warmth of scholarship instead.

In 2009, she has only been alone with Greg once. She, like the rest of her cohort, watches him from afar as he performs from his lectern. Blaine remembers, come the second year of her undergraduate degree, organising a meeting with him. Struggling with a particular assignment, she schedules a consultation in his office. She is struck by his patience, by how amenable he is to her questions. On his whiteboard, he makes branches out of phrases, and in real time she feels the muddiness of a concept become less tangled. Greg irons out the snarl of it and presents it to her in a language she can understand. This is the work of any good educator. They are honest decipherers. They peel the shield of some theory and present it to their students. They make it a thing their successors can indoctrinate themselves in.

Blaine may not have wanted Greg then, and in a lot of ways isn't even sure she ever did. But what she had wanted was wisdom, academic prowess, and this he had. The old married man could make a cantilever out of his voice, and where was the risk in that? He could bore through a line of thinking so tedious and make dramatic and rousing the most boring of theory, all while being cradled by the pillars of an audience.

Curious, I search Greg's name on YouTube, eager to find footage of a lecture of his, an example of his hoo-ha. In one video, he is in conversation with a fellow academic, a wiry man, and the two laugh over double entendres I don't understand. Greg's voice is sage and gripping. He has thick, grey hair and a gargantuan beard. Then I search Samuel's name. Then Ivan's, then Harrison's. I am their student now, parking the conversations I have with their animal parchments, eager to observe their on-paper legacy instead.

In hearing about Blaine back then, and Greg's knowledge of her—Blaine who, as a young woman, was hollow-cheeked and vulnerable when entering his orbit—I am distracted. I am forced to consider the impact of first impressions when it comes to all romantic relationships. Rose brings this to me in one of our early conversations. She had even told Samuel that her romance with him was six weeks longer than his with her, that he had—in virtue of being her tutor for a semester—earned himself a fairytale prologue and she hadn't. I love when my parents recall the story of how they met, how young and hapless they seemed then. My father, a teenager with a crush, had been strategic in teeing up a group hang at Luna Park with his best friend, his best friend's girlfriend and my mother. He had spotted her at work and was immediately spellbound. On the rotor, gravity worked its magic and plastered his face to the metal barrier, having it so he was smiling at her the entire ride. I see him in my imagination, all baby-faced and keen. Lucky for him, she was smiling back.

When connections are forged in lecture theatres between professors and their students, the origin story is hardly as cute. It is one born, instead, out of illegitimacy. The student will long wonder, as they sit in the resounding echo of what once was, when it all began. She will labour over its birthplace, will find there are no anniversaries here that aren't, at once, hitched up by student numbers and course codes.

For Elsie, Harrison does not have six weeks on her. He has eight long months. This is the amount of time he spends as her tutor before their relationship is consummated. In those eight months, there are small, safeguarded gestures. Harrison calling upon Elsie in class with a wink to offer advice and feedback to other students. And then the time, over text, both he and her organise a visit to his house for Elsie to pick up a car-full of stretched canvases, materials to assist in her honours project. She imagines it a nice home, lived-in. Stylish. What she doesn't know then is that Harrison is on the brink of a separation. That he is stuck in the twilight of a decade-long relationship, the sort filled with the labour of big, adult things, like a child and a mortgage. She learns of his failing marriage later, at one of many exhibition openings, when he is drunk. But in that moment, she assumes him happily wed and imagines—sickeningly enough—his wife opening the door to her. She hates the idea of this. Because of this, Elsie decides to take a friend. Harrison meets her at the door, and upon seeing she has company, he retrieves the canvases from the unseen part of his hallway. These lonely items, tucked into the man's grotto, are no longer able to wheedle Elsie inside as he hoped they would, for she is not alone. They will discuss this early interaction later while together in a hotel room. He will say that he was disappointed she arrived with company that day, that he was eager for the opportunity to kiss her. When she tells me this, she admits it feels quite terrible to say out loud, even just to imagine it. A tutor, twenty years her senior, masquerading an otherwise kind gesture as a window to unfurl his desires.

Does it begin at the first admission of longing? Is this when it tumbles into chaos? One evening, after an exhibition opening, Harrison and Elsie spend much of the night in arm's reach of one another, talking. The wine is free, and they drink liberally. She does not know this then, but discovers—some years later—that it is against university policy for tutors and their students to drink together. 'Most of the night is a blur and hard to describe,' she tells me. But she recalls him asking her, at one point, if she has a boyfriend. His question is the soft proof she needs to seize the moment, to avow her crush. He draws it out from her, as though this crush is attached to some small cord that only he can see. A thin rope. She only notices it then. Notices, too, how he has it wrapped around the cork of his thumb. That perhaps he has for months and months, waiting for the most opportune time to yank. Here, four beers deep, he does just that. He yanks, and yanks, and then her confession is out, eager to be rinsed of its phlegm. To be made clean. 'I have a crush on you,' she tells him softly. Everything—from that moment—changes.

Harrison turns away, as if in her admission Elsie has nailed something tremendous and ugly to the door of their relationship and he can't stand to look at it. Or perhaps it's that he can't stand to look away. He pleads aloud, to nobody in particular, that he wishes she were older, that she wasn't his student. But she isn't older, and she is his student. These are things she cannot change. It is then that he disappears into the crowd for a moment, enveloped by bodies and chatter. In her drunk stupor, she asks around for him, only for him to materialise once more in front of her, his face changed. Buoyant. He asks her if she's coming home with him *or what*, and she almost doesn't believe it, thinking him joking. But he isn't joking. His eyes are focused, and it is as if the gallery walls have disintegrated around them, where a crisp path lined with bright lights all the way to the front step of his home can be seen, tempting them both. As if he'd gone and pressed some button and made a matador of himself, bewitching her with some reddish, glaring handkerchief.

I imagine him in the interim, perhaps alone in the men's bathrooms, levelling up to his own aged reflection. Having thrown some dice, some two-faced coin, and landed on chance. On leaving-to-go-sleep-with-his-student. Elsie doesn't care what does it, what reshapes things, but loves that something has. So she follows him out of the venue and back to his home, where she climbs into his bed and, still drunk, falls asleep. In the morning, they fuck. 'It would have been one of the most intimate experiences I'd had at that age,' she tells me. At some point in the future, she will find out that another tutor present that evening took a student home as well.

Elsie, who wakes delighted in her tutor's bed that morning, both is and isn't the same woman who calls her university's Safer Communities hotline years later to consider her options in reporting an instance of sexual misconduct. One does not arrive at this verdict lightly. It hums in the background of a woman's life, a thing naked and tricky, and—once stripped of its garb—can't defend itself. Gets tongue-tied if it tries. Elsie is not a fool. She has loved and lost, and has come to learn that this relationship, in ways dissimilar to others, lacks any semblance of resolve. It is difficult to place, which begs the question: does injustice live here? Why, from this side of the fence, does it feel so wrong?

As I scour through the websites of three different Australian universities, sifting through the codes of conduct made available online, the ones that constitute sexual harassment, I am struck by the obscurity of their language, how up-in-the-air they seem. When one imagines being sexually harassed, it all seems quite deliberate: a pinch on the arse, audacious and intolerable. Being cornered in some dusty staffroom and leered at by a man with bits of bread from his lunch lodged between each tooth, who licks his lips and makes plain his big, terrible wants. They are isolated incidents. Unwanted affections. They make for a cartoonish assailant, whose features are exaggerated in all the worst places. This rendering of badness does not whisper in some corporeal language. It does not tuck a loose strand of hair behind his lover's ear and maintain she is genius.

Elsie's motivations to call Safer Communities are entirely political. After many years, she has come to consider what happened between her and Harrison symptomatic of a larger cultural mess. Yes, she was once a willing participant who had—back then—pretended not to notice the pecking order between her and her lover. But today, she cannot unsee it. Considers her interior world to have been none of her tutor's business. This, I am interested in. What leads a woman to see her love as riddled with all the wrong syllables? Who reads it again and finds it unpalatable and incorrect? These are isolating revelations. They make lonely their subjects. Rose, after nine long months of being smouldered by confirmation of having been a kind of kink, is distracted, hurt. She facetiously makes memes about horny professors, about Samuel's 'strike-rate', and sends them to me and a handful of trusted friends, paired with laughing emojis. She can't remember how it feels to not be seething all of the time. 'I feel so fucking replaceable,' she tells me.

*

Cara and her boyfriend, Richard, are ambling down Lygon Street in Carlton towards Cinema Nova one afternoon to catch a film. With his hand in hers, she spots Ivan from afar, alone and eyeballing the Readings bookshop window display across the road from the theatre. There he is, all composed and strange. He is like some darling antique, a thing she only expects to see bolstered up in a display cabinet, or lying askew on the floor of his dimly lit bedroom as he recites verses for her. Anywhere but here. There's an obscenity to it all, how tangential she is soon to become once—or if—he notices her. Here, on the street with Richard, there is no place to hide. They haven't yet crossed the road to the cinema. She can tuck her body behind the wall of some alley and wait. Wrap her scarf around her face three times. But what's worse? Him spotting her making a bolt for it, concealing herself? Retreating into the piss-end of some backstreet and catching her breath like a teenage delinquent? What then would she say to Richard, who has never heard her utter this man's name, who knows nothing of who he is, of where she's been?

'Cara,' Ivan says as she and Richard approach. 'Ivan, this is Richard,' she retorts quickly, and Richard reaches for his hand, shakes it. The interaction is brief but uncomfortable. Richard is none the wiser. After all, it's not as if Ivan is a discernible threat. He is scruffy and odd-looking, and Cara would not be surprised if, to this day, Richard had forgotten ever meeting him in the first place. 'That guy?' she imagines him asking her in mad disbelief if ever she were to mention the significance of their run-in with him. That no, they never kissed. But while collapsed in his sea of small cushions, on all of those nights when she wasn't with Richard, she ached a little for it.

As she and Richard continue towards the cinema, Cara knows that it is over with Ivan. 'From that moment, the ship had sailed,' she told me. They line up for popcorn and soda, and Cara feels a small grief rising in the pit of her stomach. Perhaps it's not Ivan she will miss. Perhaps it's the rendering of her *with* Ivan, her as some chimera, a woman aloof and baseless, that she feels the loss of. With her professor, she was nobody and somebody all at the same time. She was elsewhere, and elsewhere was not a bad place to be. In elsewhere, nobody owes anybody anything. You can glide through elsewhere with such ease, can feel the oozy tingle of being yearned for but not truly known. Elsewhere, too, where her father liked to play.

Years prior, Cara visited her family home for a few days. On one of the nights she spent there, and in a bid to make herself useful, she ordered Chinese food from a nearby restaurant. After fifteen minutes, she hopped in the car to pick it up, and her father joined. 'I'll run in and get it!' he said as they were stationed in the driveway of the eatery. He hopped out, leaving his phone face-up on the passenger seat. It buzzed, revealing a message from *My Darling.* Curious, Cara opened it. There, his elsewhere lived. There, among a torrent of lewd photographs, soft admissions of lust and tenderness, a brooding family of love hearts recycled over and over again, his elsewhere throbbed and ached. Here is where she found a woman who wasn't her mother but was his darling. It cut through Cara. Left her gaping, foaming at the mouth. He returned, followed by the waft of honest spices and some other thing, and she placed her sweaty hands on the wheel and drove. After dinner, she requested they take a walk, just the two of them. That is when she confronted him. 'I didn't want to know about the affair,' she tells me. 'And I never felt compelled to tell my mother.' Instead, the two carried on. It never came up again. Both father and daughter knew, or managed to find out, how best to place this knowledge. It was not to rear its ugly head. For Cara, what you don't know can't hurt you. To be known, and to know, is an injurious act of love. She doesn't hear from Ivan again. Not for a long time. She does not wait, or push, or ask. Instead, she closed her eyes in the cinema and squeezed Richard's hand.

*

Samuel will wake the morning after his quarrel with Rose and resume as normal. He will cast an eye over a paper and respond to a handful of emails from students, each with questions more boring than the last. He will assume Rose is asleep beneath the pleats of their doona, but she isn't. She is wide awake, unstirring. Making a detailed map of the shortfalls of this man who she had been besotted with for years. Who noticed her then and notices her still.

But somehow, he looks different to her, now that he has let slip some terrible lore. In a lot of ways, it could've been liberating, having him admit to forgetting—for a brief, clear moment—how they'd met. How, when he admitted to choking back the promise of a kiss from any old student, he surely couldn't have been talking about her. Mind you, the shadow self works in mysterious ways. It hovers over their bed and glides safely between his desk and her, the pretty wraith of who Rose was then. It says, 'Now, what makes you so special? Hmm?' Rose is a little older now, less graceful. Samuel has helped her reach for a lone back pimple before. Has found and disposed of a nail clipping. Has heard her cuss and spit and cry big tears. The sweep of their apartment is suddenly so dull, so unremarkably routine.

Rose will leave him, she decides. It is 2017. She doesn't know when or how. Just that she will. It will be messy and it will be long, and a year after their break-up, she will return to him, worn down. She will even hear him out the first time an informal complaint is filed against him in 2019 by an anonymous complainant regarding his inappropriate conduct with female students. Yes, despite offering him an ear then, she will read the complaint thrice over. Will even accidentally catch herself nodding along come the third read.

8

The man says, 'I am not as bad as the others.' There are men—larger, older, greater—who suffer from more sizeable amounts of bigotry. Men even he feels an aversion towards. Yes, these men are bad men. He has read their letters, the man says. 'So have you, I'm sure.' They are littered in every prevailing curriculum, the dispatches of these bad men. Some of these bad men are brilliant despite their burdens. This, the not-quite-good man but hardly-as-bad man, will make sure to remind you of. Yes, because some of them are idols. Some even end up effigies, all ivory and plaster. The man wants you to know that for every bad man, there is a worse man. You may even be part-bad-man yourself. 'You know, a lot of bad men are fathers,' the not-quite-good but hardly-as-bad man says. You best believe even more of them are grandfathers. Some mornings, bad men will even sway a little in their nice chairs and fight back tears. Yes, this is because bad men cry too. But the not-quite-good, hardly-as-bad man insists that when he weeps, he makes an honourable lake out of his tears. He isn't bad, but he knows bad. When Elsie is seated opposite the hardly-as-bad man at the pub on that fateful last meeting and asks him what he makes of their love, whether it is problematic, this is what he tells her. That he is, after all, hardly as bad as those bad men that came before him. 'It used to be a lot worse,' he will say doggedly.

Elliott, the retired academic I get a drink with while writing this book, carries out a similar spiel. He describes a professor—larger, older, greater, of course—who once cast his eyes on a female student at a house party the three happened to be at one evening. Elliott had noticed her too. She is described to me as someone stirring, unforgettable. She had short, dark hair and a penetrating sort of gaze, like that of a cat. Elliott would've liked to have known her. This I sniff out immediately. But the larger, older, greater man had placed his bets, and Elliott will find this out later, upon hearing that somebody spotted her leaving the larger, older, greater man's house the following morning in a T-shirt that wasn't hers. Elliott's voice is made vindictive when he tells me this. His eyes dart, and he becomes all honed and bold in how he speaks.

I find it a peculiar sort of bandaid, this one. What good does it do? Much of the world around me echoes Harrison and Elliott's sentiments. I have had many people slap me silly with rhetorical questions like: What is more concerning than professors and tutors who sleep with their students? Professors and tutors, of course, who rape their students. What is more terrible than a professor or tutor in his thirties who engages in this sort of behaviour? A professor or tutor in his fifties or sixties. I make it clear from the outset that I am not talking about certain tyrannies and hate that this is something I feel compelled to specify. But this is what the fallacy of relative privation demands. It levels its finger at some faraway crumminess, a badness on the edge of a lonely field, and insists that that *there*, that tiny speck with its tiny shanks, is what we ought to be focusing on instead.

The student, in all of these instances, is the elephant in the room. She balloons outwards, her love a thing as big and punishing as they come, and she can't help but scrape her leathery bits on every bend in the wall, every recess. And somehow, she *is* every bend, every recess. Harrison will peek out from between Elsie's arms every so often and ask her if she is okay, if it has all become a bit cramped in this wedging space. But he doesn't care for her response, can't hear it from where he is shrouded. She is forced now to hide, made all the worse in that he can see her hiding, has found arousing the lying low of it all. He won't ever say it aloud, how hot it inevitably becomes. The young girl, masquerading as his mentee, is always going to be both two-thirds forbidden, one-third not. After they sleep together the first time, they agree not to do it again, as if what was meant to be unknown can retreat back into limbo once more. It doesn't pan out that way, unsurprisingly. They spend months cavorting between various accommodations. As his divorce makes headway, he arranges to stay at a friend's abode in Carlton.

Elsie appreciates the change of scenery. She hates the knowledge of having rolled about in another woman's sheets so soon after her separation. There are other apartments and hotels and small, rootless homes, moments Elsie will later describe as 'snatched'. She was adamant about never leaving a toothbrush, or a bobby-pin, or an earring, or any small semblance of her body having rubbed clean against the furniture of an unfamiliar space.

She arrives at university one afternoon and spots Harrison in the passageway. She had been with him until noon that same day and, despite heading back home, hadn't had time to shower. She had only returned home to pick something up before heading into class. This means that when she appears in the corridor before him, she is in the outfit she'd worn to his house the night prior. Harrison, on the other hand, is in fresh clothes. She describes this moment to me as 'enormously charged', as if crushed into both sleeves of his blazer are two Harrisons: the untouchable expert, and the man who had closed his eyes and nuzzled into her embrace just hours earlier. It's not necessarily the charge of a secret that leaves an imprint on her, but some other thing: the presence of his vulnerability, and in turn, the luxury of it having afforded her a new kind of bionic vision. Of being able to spot something fresh and exciting in him, something she'd unearthed from the heart of their shared campus. Later, unable to leave his barracks, he will hand her twenty dollars and ask her to fetch him a bite. She will return with his food and hand him back the note in full.

Samuel, too, is a hardly-as-bad sort of man. In fact, over the span of their relationship, he will insist to Rose that he is exceptionally good, and she will believe him. By twenty-one, she develops a keen interest in gender studies. She likes how it makes quiet deities out of people not dissimilar to her, women throughout history blunted by prejudice, and she chooses to study these women keenly. That same year, she is quick to unhand herself of her double major. This, she insists, is a gesture she willingly embarks upon alone, a loving rite of passage. It is a sacrifice made shy in that she does not busy Samuel with her concerns, does not care to have him burdened by her offering. She reasons with herself that by deciding not to major in philosophy any longer, she is able to circumvent the risk of being Samuel's student again and can alleviate him of the complex task of managing a conflict of interest. Yes, she is a student at her particular institution. But she is also a tutor's girlfriend at that same institution, and this requires governance. Nobody ever thinks to ask her why she does this. Her family wouldn't know how to scrutinise her, now that she has ventured into uncharted territory. They work, instead, with their hands.

Rose will bring ideas to Samuel and rip through the fibrousness of feminist theory for him. The tendons of a concept will unfurl themselves at their shared desk, and he will look upon each one, impressed. It is then that Rose notices the shape of his projects changing. They are slowly becoming more hers. How riveting it all feels at the time for her to have influenced him in such a way. For Rose to notice him as he finds, lodged between each tooth, a fine-grained thought of hers, only to pick it out, inspect it further. How quickly then does his career materialise, and before long he is lecturing on the subject, even speaking on academic panels—typically, might I add, reserved for women—about the virtues and ruinations of gender theory. Most mornings, Rose drives to the nearby cafe she works at while she completes her degree. But she cherishes their nightly conversations. Considers herself fortunate to be with a man as plugged-in and progressive as he is. Later she will consider it a kind of plagiarism, and only then will she want to rip the coronet from his head and insist him a fraud.

The hardly-as-bad man, in his good-man appointment, will fetch for Rose the secrets of other women. Women like Ellen. Ellen entrusts him with a quiet, guarded truth. She confesses to having been the object of her high-school teacher's fantasy way back when. She trusts him, and he likes this. He will bring these offerings to Rose, will ask her to disassemble them with him. This is a language she excelled in: the dialect of other, worse men. He will even, upon being trusted with information about another tutor at his university who had exploited his position to get into bed with a student of his, schedule a meeting on campus with some department head and raise his concerns with them. Samuel decides that men who leave women to stagger in their wake will become his enemy. With Rose, he is brandished a prophet. Yet all the while, he will speak over her. 'That doesn't sound correct, Rose,' he will say, and she will think, *You are not a fucking God.* But in her frustration, she will edify him further, equip him with more feminist material. Like the time she gifted him a book about how women speak, about how—in classroom settings—they are routinely hushed. How obvious, I think. For her to have the two of them return to the classroom once more. The book detailed how women find themselves catching their breath among the louder, more reverberant claims of their male peers. He reads it. And for this, she is grateful. Later, he will attach a precursor to an email. He will send it out before the start of each semester. His class disclaimer will tap into the hearts of his female undergraduates. It says that yes, he has done the readings. Yes, he knows that women are habitually silenced, and because of this he will make a concerted effort in every tutorial to encourage his female students to speak. I offer this anecdote up to an academic from Perth as part of my research. They will find this gesture suspicious. They will point out that in Samuel's deed, even the most self-willed of his female students may feel indebted to him, as if only he has granted them permission to express themselves.

*

When Blaine is asked about bad men, there are many that come to mind. But there is one in particular—Cameron—whose outline is as stiff and severe in her memory as was his body on the evening he assaulted her. During the tail-end of her affair with Greg, she had been introduced to Cameron through her brother. Blaine had found many of his characteristics inexcusable right from the outset. Like how he'd boast about cheating on every single girlfriend he'd had, and how he'd unapologetically plagiarised his way through a business degree. Lori, too, insisted he was insincere. After one particular dinner party, Lori had noticed how Cameron had spent the evening prying the secrets of his guests, all the while not offering anything substantial about himself. But he was handsome and mischievous and looked at Blaine with hungry, wanton eyes. She knew he wasn't the kind of man she cared to fall in love with. That would be too slippery, too foolish. But here—from this other, smaller place—she doesn't hate his company. Can make do with some relic of affection, the occasional pleasure of flattery. She could follow Cameron in and out of restaurants, and with him she had an excuse to paint her lips for once.

One evening, after a routine meal together, he had accompanied her back home. He closed her front door behind him with marked force. Before long, the bad-man yanked a little at the zip of her jeans and began to make a torn canopy out of her lips. She'd mumbled something then, let fall from her mouth a scant, tiny racket. An *oh* that could've been a *no* if he'd thought to ask. If he'd paused between each hot breath and asked her, 'Sorry, did you say something, Blaine?' Politely, she shuffled her body. She made a meek bid to delay the inevitable, to not let him forge a mess of her. No, this is not what she wants. *Oh,* again—only once he'd sidled inside, once he'd irrupted in all of the places he shouldn't have, and so she clenched her teeth a little and reasoned with herself. *Well,* she thought. *There's the line. And here it is, crossed.* This line: a thing that had found itself twisted, like twine inside the small of her gut. Something frayed and sad.

The violation stays, just long enough. The night after, Blaine feels its terrible nag, how eagerly it climbs into bed with her. She does not cry out when it does but lays next to it, pretending not to count its deep, quick inhales. Blaine is careful. She does not let her lungs strain to the shape of its panting, will not match its cadence. If this means she is to hold her breath, she will. When she wakes in the morning, she is awash with misplaced guilt, common for many survivors of sexual assault. She takes the violation to Greg as if it is something he ought to know. After all, he had been curious about Cameron. She'd mentioned Cameron before, and had even told Greg that she found him attractive.

Upset, Greg responds to her news by arriving at her doorstep. He does a terrible job of veiling his hurt. She is his plaything, the gofer to his carnal errands, and he is—because he has decided—a hardly-as-bad sort of man. The hardly-as-bad man can piggyback the bad-man, who destroys the earth with his big, bad shoes. All the while, the hardly-as-bad man will not have his feet soiled or scraped. The woman, already hollowed out, is not to know the difference.

Greg will force Blaine to fuck him that day. He will ask her if Cameron used a condom, and it will be the first time he pauses before not using one himself. He will fuck her with might, fasten his big hands around her shoulders when he does, as if to leave an obvious set of handprints. He will fuck her, and then he will leave. But she will have already left, having ventured into numbness the moment the hardly-as-bad man makes bad his wants. Will be gone where nothing—and no-one—can touch her. She hears the door close when he does leave and is swallowed up by the stillness of her home, by the thing she cannot name. It is then that she rolls onto her side and howls.

*

I am endeavouring to untwist two knots—the question of whether or not pedagogical relationships are proof of an exceptional love, found in the wrong place at the wrong time, or just exceptionally bad teaching practices—both of which have found themselves tangled in the same dishonourable heap. Amia Srinivasan unravels it better in her book *The Right to Sex* when she asks, in considering the ethics of professors sleeping with their students, if the question 'isn't whether "real" romantic love is possible in the pedagogical context, but whether real teaching is'. I am struck by the efforts many women in these relationships make when it comes to deciding whether or not their teachers, who later are to become their lovers, are bad. It seems a strange, almost laborious task to have to undergo as students. These four women aren't meant to know, or care, if these men are good men. It shouldn't bother them, least of all still. If Harrison had arrived before Elsie as a mere conduit of knowledge, scrubbed and at the ready, she would not find herself irate. Would not end up standing on some street corner in Brunswick, damp with angry sweat and knowing, all the while, that he has tasted the salt of it a generous handful of times. If Samuel had anchored himself only to his craft, he would've betrayed no-one, least of all Rose. If Greg had cared only to bestow onto Blaine the mechanics of a well-formed sentence, of syntax, he would've pardoned her long ago, would've saved her the undue punishment. Even Ivan, who renders Cara a question mark in and of herself, whose job was never to leave his student treading in uncertain waters, always and forever unsure of the depth. How unnecessarily near these four women are to these men, how close. It goes without saying that they too weren't meant to be known, to be felt in such ways. *Yes, of course it does.* I have known many women, myself included, who have had to grapple with whether or not the men in their life have perpetrated ill behaviour or continue to. Unfortunately, that is the labour of love, particularly heterosexual love that blooms out of the soil of a patriarchal society. But to do all of this heavy-lifting, or rather to be expected to teach men, in a lot of ways, how best to behave while in the shadow of having once been their student, feels grossly weighted in the wrong person's favour.

But I am reminded of being of a child in primary school, of spotting a teacher on the weekend as she peruses the aisles of her local shopping centre. Here, she minds her own business and still appears to me as alien, a person I can't quite catalogue if not standing before me, and the rest of her class, during homeroom. I am distracted, almost transfixed by the novelty of it all. For she is unveiled in the real world, and I—unsure how to be—can't help but notice.

9

I WAKE IN THE night to a terse bark. It is a brief hostility and, given I know the language of my dog's growls, I can safely presume its cause. It is the sound he makes when my cat gets in his way. Perhaps she had slithered atop of his bed, or brushed up against his hindquarters as he endeavoured to sleep. It is a single, sharp holler, and then it is done. This is how Fil complains. He offers his enemy a lone threat by baring his teeth just once. 'What do you think animals are trying to communicate when they complain?' I ask Jade, a friend of mine, later that day. 'Distance,' she offers.

If you spoil an animal's peace, they will pin back their ears, or raise their hackles, or make loud their dislike. Their body will surrender its tolerance. The animal will impart on their antagonist a simple task: to back off. Space is what the cat craves when, mid-pat, her eyes widen, her body stiffens and she sings for you some terrible mewl. How inborn this need is, for one to carve out distance if slighted.

This animal want is never met if one embarks upon an institutional complaints process. Once Rose sends the first email to Safer Communities, she will be forced to endure a wicked closeness to her grievance, will be made to lodge each of her snarls, to package them. Here, in the heart of her complaint, is where she will be forced to live.

In a lot of ways, a formal complaints process has no end date. Rose will log her accusation in December 2023, and by the time I write this, nearly a year later, it will still be stalled. It will be made cruel in its dustiness. Perhaps it has hurtled forward. But she isn't to know this. No-one will call her. Maybe, she thinks, this is because what happened to her isn't deemed important. Because of this, she isn't even sure herself if what happened *is* important. If anything happened at all. But she is distracted by Samuel's repute in the academy, his good name. She will entertain broadcasting an old-fashioned callout, will consider tagging his place of work in a tweet. But she can't stomach the thought of refreshing her feed just to see who has noticed.

Ellen, who is more astute, takes the lead. She knocks on office doors and neatly arrange her concerns into pithy, indelicate emails. She requests little, but requests it nonetheless. She and Rose even travel to Rose's old university campus to meet with an established feminist academic based there and ask for guidance. The three of them discuss the matter over coffee. Rose's drink ventures down the wrong hole after taking her third sip, and she chokes a little at the table. She splutters fiercely between coughs and notices Ellen looking on, embarrassed. How crude and base it all seems, to find oneself retching in between protest. To need to stand and spit out the milky remains of one's coffee in a nearby bush. It is only in this moment, when Rose's body momentarily forgets how to swallow, that she feels the obvious embarrassment of this process. It is so obstructive.

There are many phone calls and even more emails. Rose reaches out to Josephine, the head of school at a university she never attended, to piggyback complaints that Ellen had made against Samuel there. This man, she tells her, has slept with three students at three different institutions. 'I was one of them,' she says. She signs off each letter, declaring herself an expert in him. Rose becomes familiar with a tired script, a concise, 300-word rundown of the last decade of her life. Josephine, upon receiving Rose's email, calls her immediately. She tells Rose she is brave. This is how she butters her up. Josephine insists that, with her, the injustice will be neatly rectified. She will thank Rose for undressing it, for lifting its stout arms above its head and making a map out of its birthmarks. By the time Josephine hangs up, Rose is almost rapt. She doesn't know then that Josephine will have spent forty long minutes constructing a mirage, and Rose—thirsty, and desperate—will have bought it.

Over the span of a year, the mirage will become more obvious. Josephine stops answering Rose's calls or responding to her emails. She smiles uncomfortably at Ellen if ever she sees her in one of the university lifts. But Rose is lucky, given she has Ellen. Ellen is principled and circumspect. She will not sprinkle salt into any good wound just because.

With Ellen, a formal complaints process ensues. She arrives before an investigator, a twenty-five-year-old woman with a slicked-back ponytail who works in the university's Human Resources team. Here, in the eyes of a Human Resources complaint, Ellen is a legitimate witness in that she is not cast as Samuel's scorned ex-girlfriend. The investigator makes no long-winded promises, and for this Ellen is grateful. She has grown tired of Josephine's hyperbole and will come to resent how she swans about on campus, volunteers secrets from her own life to imply solidarity. 'Yes, when I was a student,' Josephine has told her, recalling hideous stories of sexual misconduct she had witnessed, or perhaps even weathered herself, way back when.

What is postured as a swift two-week inquest quickly turns into a two-month ordeal. Then six. By the ninth month, nobody is counting. Rose instead keeps a tally of justice's little ripples. She becomes some kind of desert dweller, yearning for justice, parched and prowling towards a big body of water that may or may not exist. She has been warned of this juncture many a time by women not too dissimilar to her. At this juncture, justice becomes an apparition. This is because, for every man who keeps his job, a woman is burdened with another, more back-breaking job: the job of becoming his complainant.

*

In the process of writing this book, Cara calls me, amused. This is because, for the first time in nearly four years, she has received a message from Ivan. She can sniff on him the scent of a breakup. 'Bonjour,' it reads. I notice something shift in her voice when she recites their message exchanges. She puts me on speakerphone and scrolls through their conversations. She has returned to the sandbank of her fantasies. She will make a penpal out of him once more. The mirage is all she needs.

I ask Cara about daydreams and receive, in response, a love letter to the art of reverie. Every day, she will carve out time just to muse. She takes a long seaside walk, allowing the whirring throb of what-could-be occupy her mind. When she was a student, she would regularly order a coffee at an on-campus cafeteria, where a particular album would play from their speaker. She remembers asking the barista the name of it and later listening to it repetitively. She doesn't tell me the title of the album, despite me asking. In a lot of ways, it doesn't matter, and—in even more ways—I am unsurprised. Cara has long kept classified the loose teachings of her recipes, the ones that make up such wishful thinking. Every time she listens to this album, her mind will work its magic. She conjures up an image of herself back then, young and dawdling down the corridor, before entering Ivan's class. When the key changes or a bridge resounds or the fourth song pulsates with a familiar drumbeat, she closes her eyes. The soft haze of her memory will have it so she is opening his classroom door. And then, between big blinks, Cara will see him smiling.

In the business of chimera, anything is possible. There is no consequence, no hurt. There are no storms, and even if there were, the lawns would not be wet afterwards, the roofs of cars not hollowed out by the snapped limbs of big trees. The canals here don't overflow. This, Cara has mastered. She has learned not to let the mirage of her wants interfere with real life. Real life is a different beast altogether. It reaps the repercussions of bad behaviour, and when it comes to real life, one cannot simply close their eyes and start again. Cara, awaken by guilt one morning many years ago, will wish to do just this: to start again. Alistair, the man who lies naked next to her as he sleeps, is unkind and vain. But worse than this, he is not her boyfriend. Her boyfriend is somewhere else, asleep and none the wiser. He will awake instead in some neighbouring suburb, awaiting Cara's return from a sleepover.

When Cara meets Alistair a month or so prior, she is taken aback. He has cold, steel eyes and an unanswerable aura. It is as if nobody has ever told him no, least of all a woman. He wears extortionately priced slacks and irons his T-shirts. Alistair lives in an industrial penthouse in the heart of Fitzroy. Here, he sears wagyu on the pan and makes his guests woozy with full-bodied cabernet sauvignon, if they aren't already tingling from the cocktail of prescription drugs and cocaine on offer. One night, Cara arrives at Alistair's with her friend, Ben. Seated around the dinner table already are a handful of misfits, all kneading the legs and arms and cheeks of one another. The house felt muscular with promise then, as if everybody were throbbing a little beneath the belt.

'Who are these people?' she asks Alistair, unsettled. He holds her gaze a moment and grins. 'I don't know, really. I met them at the pub earlier.' Caught then between awe and unease, she decides it best to leave.

He wants her, and she likes this. Given she is in a relationship with somebody else, she revels instead in fantasy, imagines—when she's alone—being touched by Alistair, opening her mouth for him. He has troubling, big hands that yearn for her, and she has a body that would hurl itself into his if given the chance. But she doesn't need the promise of the act itself to enjoy it. Her mind does all of the heavy lifting, offers her a screenplay instead. Cara knows that to have the best of both worlds, it is imperative that neither bleeds into the other. She does not care to lick the wounds of something pious and doomed. She knows not to goad the wild brute of her desires. If she is to offer it a wide berth, it will not need to slice her clean. Alistair, on the other hand, is less satiated. His imagination is not half as titillating. He carries on, obedient only to his wants. If he is to leave his mark, he will, considering the stain of it only thereafter. So, he does. He persists and persists and persists some more, and there are weeks of it: of raw, obvious persistence. One evening, he will put his lips on her, and she—worn down by then, but still eager—will relent. When he fucks her, it is rough and heady, and she will feel smudged by it, by the merciless way in which he peels her legs apart. Perhaps this is how Cara's two worlds haemorrhage together. In entering Cara, Alistair will accidentally pierce through the comforts of her fantasy land. Real-life Alistair will look around and make a terrible mess of it. She wants to tell real-life Alistair that it is best he go, that this is where she plays. But by then, he will have already left, and his mirage is nowhere to be seen. She will close her eyes that evening, as her boyfriend reads a chapter of his book in bed next to her, and won't be able to conjure up a single thing. The desert of her mind is too arid now, too lonely. This, she does not care to lose. So she decides then, that in order to indulge in daydream, she will not muddy her worlds. A few months later, enrolled in Ivan's class, her wants will return. She will plug in her headphones and soundtrack her thirst. She will return to herself unscathed.

*

Despite having attended a different university, when Elsie tells me about her experience with Safer Communities, it echoes Rose's. There, between the surge of sweet talk, they cast for her a similar mirage of justice. Elsie, unlike Rose, had no intention to make certified her concerns. She did want to put Harrison's relationship with her on the most draconian of ice, to have it labelled and numbered in some chock-full university freezer. She isn't even sure the hardly-as-bad man will do it again if given the chance. Because of this, the resolution she cares for is not penance. It is something softer, more generous. She wants her university to be a place she, as an older woman, will come to miss. For the husk of its beautiful, big buildings to evoke nostalgia in her, if ever she were to hurry past it during a morning commute. She wants real, lasting change. None of this bad-apples bullshit. For her, Harrison's desires did not prick through the meshwork of an institution, did not make for a pronounced hole in the trellis. Yes, he may have peered through it, and this may have been ill-advised. Wrong, even. But Elsie has come to understand his wants as systematic. She is the mud wedged between the furrows of his sneakers. And he is only a man, after all. A tutor encouraged, like all of the others, to dance about in the dirt with his students. With few boundaries between faculty staff and the people they teach, somebody is bound to slip into the sludge of it all. To cake their hands with its mess.

Her wants are too woolly, too sweeping, for Safer Communities to consider. They expect her to report him, to have her grievance typed up, printed and pinned like a crinkled-up donkey's tail to Harrison's back. Given that her requests are to anonymously encourage stricter boundaries between students and teachers, they would involve quite a large and sweeping upheaval. But to pin him as having done the wrong thing and not having acted simply in accordance with what the lax environment permitted would be less effort. This is easier, more administrative. She fantasises instead about writing a letter. About delivering it anonymously to her institution. How rewarding, for it to blazon throughout the school community, creased in fours and photocopied, so every student can mull over its truth. She imagines it read by honours students who think twice the next time they feel compelled to pour out and onto their tutors. She sees it mulled over by professors, who feel a pang of indignity if they are to recall the last time they clinked glasses with a young hopeful at a boozy exhibition opening, whose eyes were as fuzzy as they were anticipative. She wants the account of her life to have an aftertaste, for its leftovers to nourish a cohort of young painters. Very quickly does she learn that the justice she desires cannot be acquired through such formal channels. So she retires her wants and retreats again into the solitude of unpacking this mess alone.

For a student to feel entitled to justice, they must first feel entitled to receiving care. While facilitating a writers' workshop recently, I find myself intrigued by one particular anecdote a student of mine offers up, a story from her own life. She tells me about herself as a child who, in a bid to protect her most prized possession—a limited edition Barbie doll—she, at seven years old, made sure it remained always in the refuge of its box. Because to care for something does not always mean to fiddle with it, to paw at its plastic limbs. To roll up its small cotton sleeves and cut triangles out of its tulle skirt, no matter how compelled. At twenty, while a student of literature myself, and a week after a cousin of mine had suicided, I handed in a poorly written assignment.

I had endeavoured to compose an instructive report on a novella I had forgotten to read, given how swallowed up at the time I was by grief and that other hideous thing: guilt, as is often the case with suicide. The looming overhang of many an unanswered question. I failed, but upon receiving my marks, was sent an email from my tutor asking to meet with me, eager to discuss it.

I braved his office the next day, embarrassed. I had not requested an extension, had not thought to. My tutor was an older man with a stern demeanour, so when he carefully pried out the particulars of my life then, he did not volunteer the warm cradle of his big arms. Did not offer a shoulder. No, he cared not to lean forward and request I weep and splutter into him, did not hope I'd leave a teardrop—something small and felt—on his shoulder, something that had leaked out of me and onto him. Instead, he adjusted my mark just enough so as not to have it spoil my grade point average. This was how he endeavoured to make fair something terribly unfair, how he cared. He did it in all of the afar ways he could.

My student, in recalling the memory about her Barbie doll, continues. She tells me that on her eighth birthday, her father had requested she bring her treasured asset to him, that he and her mother had planned for her a surprise. They had baked a Barbie cake and thought it would be sweet if her favourite doll were seated atop of the flour castle they had carefully assembled together. My student excitedly handed her father the Barbie. But in a bid to make the doll fit into the cake, he pried apart her smooth plastic legs, yanking each one off in swift, cruel tugs. My student screamed, not expecting her doll to be cleaved of her bottom half, to be ruined from the waist down. But her father, confused, had imagined the doll's torso placed atop a sugary pink gown so the icing dress ballooned out from her midriff. This is how he thought to care, by snapping his daughter's doll in two.

I am sure that if my tutor had shepherded me into his arms that day and held me, I would've appreciated the gesture. When all's said and done, what's so wrong about a hug? Perhaps if he had thought to check on me a week or a month later, I would've delighted in his concern. Maybe, in feeling beholden to him then, I would've asked him about himself a little, would've inquired. But in keeping me encased in the security of a healthy grade point average, he offered me something no friend could afford. They had arms to slump into and shoulders to cry on. He, on the other hand, had power, had influence. This is how he ought to have cared, and this is how he did care. As, and only ever as, my teacher.

10

WHEN BLAINE NOTICES GREG'S newfound interest in Jenna, she becomes a woman possessed. She finds Jenna's Facebook page and trails the comments Greg leaves on every photograph of her young student. Here, she looks for clues, for something suspect. She paranoically logs his online movements. James, her boyfriend, will bear her research. Some days, he will receive a gamut of screenshots and be made to sieve through them for badness. He will be at work, and she will be sifting through the map of Greg's online indiscretions with a red marker and a keen want. 'Look!' And then there will be something else. A small flirtation, a wink where there shouldn't have been one. Jenna is fresh-faced and idealistic and likes to post photos of her day: a cappuccino she has ordered ('Careful not to burn your lips! ;P'), a bird she has spotted whose wings she finds pretty ('That bird knows how to flaunt its feathers ... just like someone else I know'), an exhibition she has attended ('I hope you took advantage of the free wine, miss'). James wishes Blaine would just leave it, that she'd sober up of Greg's influence. He thinks Greg vile, dull and obvious. 'Yes, of course it's suspicious.' Over dinner, Blaine will bore James with her entreaties, will ask him what Greg could possibly mean when he left on Jenna's photograph a comment as oblique as that one, or as teasing at this one, and James will not necessarily know what to do with them. James knows what Greg means, and so does Blaine.

You're not meant to litter a new relationship with crud from the old. But I've come to learn, while writing this book, that relationships such as these don't abide by such manners. They implore being looked at, considered for years after. They lack the resolve of a breakup and make long-tired sleuths out of their subjects, eager always for answers. These men become course codes. Dishonest assignments in and of themselves. What are their prerequisites, I wonder? Perhaps that is how Blaine feels. As if she, to Jenna, is a prerequisite of Greg's. The proviso of his gross desires. Was it that he had done this before? Is that why he was so adept at slotting himself into her twenty-five-year-old student trajectory?

The first time I speak with Blaine, it is over Zoom. James pops in occasionally to bring her dinner and then later dessert. He will help her throughout the course of this endeavour. He will even teach her how to export years and years of Facebook messages with Greg for me to ferret through. He will insist, though, at a few heavy junctions, that she might be better absconding herself from this mess, that she will become hot and bothered if forever stuck in the belly of this beast. I don't disagree with him. I have watched women empty the pockets of their lives only to be left with nothing more than the morsel of an old tissue. I have observed as women have made cold skeletons of themselves. Women who have submitted to some aloof, governing body and been ignored. Is there a name for a phenomenon such as this, of being made—over time—nothing more than a debased legacy?

The first time I meet Georgie's father, Tony, it is over dinner to celebrate his sixty-fifth birthday. We meet at a restaurant in Sydney's east, and he is donned in a thin gunmetal scarf and offbeat leather brogues. He is bountiful in how he greets me, kind. I know, because Georgie has told me about a significant relationship in Tony's life: him, at seventeen years old, having fallen in love with a teacher at his school. Nora, this teacher, was young, but not young enough. For nine years, she led him into the rich undercarriage of Sydney's arts culture, made a man out of him. When he asks me what I'm working on, I tell him about this book. I do it carefully, concealing its prudence, as I don't know yet how he feels about the matter. More than this, I don't know how he feels about himself as a young adult, about Nora. His ears are pricked nonetheless. When he admits to having had a relationship with his teacher, he does so coyly. The night ensues and, over wine, other past relationships of his are recalled, all falling neatly under the moniker of 'ex'. But for Nora, it's different. It's as if 'ex' is too honourable a label. No, an 'ex' is a kind of ode, proof of a relationship that, at one stage, was able to stand on its own two feet. You can drive away from an 'ex', can pack your car with the crates of what once was and sob or cheer or stare vacuously forward, casting one's eyes upon a lonely road instead. With an 'ex', you can be made rinsed with time. Nora, instead, is Tony's 'teacher-lady'. This is how he refers to her, when I ask about her specifically, about his ex-partner. He corrects me. No, Nora wasn't his 'ex', she was his 'teacher-lady'. Yes, they spent nine long years together. But she was his teacher-lady. What, then, was he to her? This, I am not sure of. I wonder if that's why these labels melt off of the chassis of these relationships, why they can't seem to stick. Is it that the young man, who was once her student, awakes one day and finds that he is unable to be categorised? Is he her 'ex', or is he her symptom?

For Rose, Samuel—despite having been her boyfriend—is not an 'ex' either. She and Ellen refer to him as a 'studentfucker'. They cackle when they do. They tell me that a studentfucker is like a motherfucker, just more precise. For as long as he remains on his carousel of student romances, he will never be her ex. Samuel, in procuring a relationship with Sienna, is a man eager to gut the fish of his wants, to remove its sharp bones before he digs in, but Rose will not let him. She *is* the sharp bones, the scrag he pulls the muscle and fat off of. 'There are plenty of fish, and you chose me again,' she thinks. 'At least she wasn't from the same school,' she thinks again. In this way, Rose is both resurrected and never laid to rest in the first place. Like a ghost who blows hot air out from beneath a curtain. This is how she makes a thing go whoosh. A ghost who toys with an electric socket. She is here on mission. She hopes to haunt him in much the same way he haunts her. Rose does not care to afford him the title of being an 'ex' as—to her—it appears he is in the same, hollow relationship he was in before. I have no doubts it's different, because of course it is. Because Sienna is distinct, with her own loveable quirks. There are things she likes that Rose doesn't. Things she hates. Rose may even be one of those things that she hates. But Sienna's body moves on its own. This, Rose accepts as true, although I feel compelled to remind her. Yes, she is sure that Sienna is endearing and special, and that as a teenager her bedroom walls were fitted out with different crinkled posters from that of Rose's. There are songs she listens to religiously that Rose has never heard of, songs—perhaps—she has introduced to Samuel. But none of this matters to Rose, as

Samuel has rendered Sienna numerical, has made her part of his dirty rotten index.

Tony once told me about one particular night some years ago. In his memory, he is distracted while listening to talkback in the early hours of the morning. He is kept company by the imperturbable words of some ABC presenter, who mulls kindly over Nick Kyrgios. On the air, the presenter considers the long, knotty lines of his life, his triumphs and setbacks. He occasionally reads aloud a text he receives from the public, some cut-off chunk of sentimentality from his listeners. Tony has almost tuned out when a message from a woman named Nora, in a suburb less than five kilometres from his, is read aloud. Nora, the ABC presenter notes, is a fan of Kyrgios. She considers him misunderstood and impressive. She valiantly comes to his defence. Tony feels in him a familiar mist, a murk of suspicion, when he hears this. He types out a message to his English teacher from way back when, his teacher-lady, something along the lines of, 'I see you're still a fan of young Greek boys'. The letters will be gobbled up by many a backspace, and then his testimony will disappear. He could make a thing go whoosh if he wanted to, could strain his body into a knowing wink if so compelled. But it may not have even been her. What is Tony to do with her apparition? He decides then that his words will not rust in her inbox. He turns off the radio and takes himself to bed.

A month or so after Blaine introduces Jenna to Greg, he starts to remind her at every junction. She receives a text from him out of the blue, saying something like: 'Oh, how lovely. I just opened my phone to a really nice message from Jenna'. Late one afternoon, she is marking papers in her office, and he barges in excitedly with his son. His kid plays with the velcro strap of his backpack while his father cavorts about the workspace. Greg scans the office. He bores Blaine as he makes small talk with the other academics. Then he exhales, glances down at his watch, and says to his son, 'We best be off, Jenna will be on her way to our place for dinner.' This is how he disrupts Blaine's peace, how he never seems to leave her alone. She looks down at the ceaseless pile of essays before her then and becomes stumped for a moment, unsure as to how Greg—as a young academic himself, all those years ago—thought to declare his university a place he'd circle romance around, the most appropriate arena to make pronounced his desires. Blaine's classes do not throb with anticipation. She does not pull her students in by the waist and insist they take a long, hot gander at her. Does not take her pick. There is no student waiting for her at home, and this is not something she believes deserving of some wreath. This is just how it ought to be, how it is for her and many she knows. It can be a gesture so swift they may not notice she has done so. But Blaine notices these things. When Greg fiddles with his keys and waits a moment for the fresh zest of cologne to dry on his neck before Jenna arrives on his doorstep that evening, Blaine will notice it on him the next time she sees him. He is as trite, as rehearsed, as he has always been. She will wait a week, will let the man dig his own shallow grave. Then she will let him have it. If he is to make a lesson out of her, she will ensure it be learned.

*

Study, for Elsie, is a saving grace. For as long as she can remember, she has been clever. As a child, she received the highest marks in her year and spent a designated chunk of her youth abroad, completing her tuition in France. By the time she turned seventeen, she had ruminated in more than one language, bookmarked many a page in her mind in different vernaculars.

As we speak, she sips whisky from her faded chair. She is twenty-eight years old. It is a little before midnight, and she is in a chalet in Italy's countryside, finessing a grant application. Elsie has long been studious. But after her father's death, she needed study in a way she hadn't before. She needed a thing to call in the night, to have it answer. To learn, as in to labour over scholarship, is to remove oneself from the gloom of one's surroundings, to momentarily abscond oneself from the gag of grief. She is sure, by the time her honours project is completed, she will return to her broken heart changed and have found—in her thesis's end, or in some administrative timestamp—the suit of armour she needs to come back to her sadness. It is then that she will make sense of it again, and it will have aged, not as tart and bloody as it was when she left it. Elsie knows that one isn't ever able to take leave from an anguish as decisive as this, but if she can fill the silence of her days with erudition, the load will lighten.

Grief such as this struggles to dry. And even if it does, it makes clefts out of the surface it hardens onto. If you *are* the surface, every time you move, a chink of grief will move with you, will splinter onto the ground where you stand, nagging you to clean it. To lose a parent at such a young age is to find oneself ruptured. There will be seats made empty at every jamboree from here on end. Milestones left docked. At every new dogleg, every uncharted corner in the road, you will arrive changed. With each plane ride, or framed degree, or suckling mass of baby, or accumulation of debt or heartache or something else entirely, you will want to introduce yourself to your beloved dead parent again, just to say, 'See? I did it. You did it. Everything is okay, or it will be soon, like you said.'

One such jamboree for Elsie is her graduation. Once she hangs her honours project from a wide, plain display wall, her mother will join her afterwards at the post-graduation party her university puts on. The night is a roaring success, and Elsie is proud. Her mother watches on as Elsie is commemorated in her big, black robes. While the two sink glasses of champagne, Harrison approaches. Her mother stands, beaming beside her daughter. Harrison tells her mother that he thinks Elsie is magnificent. 'Your daughter is astonishing,' he will declare humbly. Elsie notices. She is flattened in that small instance. Reduced momentarily to a meaty A+, this man's rubber-stamp. She can't wear his words tonight. Can only conceive of herself, months earlier, collecting every last small thing of hers after one of their evenings together. In her memory, she makes a concerted effort to leave his room traceless, before tiptoeing out into the courtyard, away from the bare, makeshift home he sleeps in. Yet here he lets his hot breath settle onto her mother's cheek, like a thing she'd earned. He is hardly nervous. He grips his beer and does not budge. He smiles a big, emphatic smile. Does he not know that women pick up on these things? That Elsie's mother had been able to count how many underhanded confessions her daughter had made throughout the year? Oh, how Elsie would talk wildly of this man, of all the bellowing wants he could help her master. She had, as mothers do, sniffed on her daughter a crush.

When a person decides to attend university, this decision can be made complex. They may be the first-in-the-family, may find themselves under one's own steam as they navigate weird, online interfaces that make for gibberish, as they decrypt the language of scholarship. Or they may have been bred for this, taking part in the lore of their household. Doing as is and has always been done when it comes to their lineage. It is very rarely a willy-nilly decision, particularly if one is to consider the burden of a HECS bill. Some of us may enrol in a course in the hopes that we will find ourselves and—if we're lucky—a vocation along the way. Every university advertisement will swank on about opportunities: the opportunity to travel, to network, to foster a career, a purpose. When Harrison tells Elsie, during their last conversation, that yes, he had had opportunities to pursue relationships with students before her, she scowls. Her world is rendered small because of him, made frivolous.

I am reminded of a simple, tangible truth that drifts above this book every so often. That no student goes to university to fuck their professor. If we are to accept otherwise, we are to curtail the strides it takes for many people—women in particular—to equip themselves with hard-earned degrees. To consider a student an opportunity in and of herself is to erase her of the saga of her life. Does an opportunity have opportunities? Is an opportunity anything but a vehicle—a time or set of circumstances—that summons the company of he who thinks to seize it? Is Elsie meant to cheer for him, this man who had admitted to having closed a window or two, despite having felt the cool breeze of its opening, having heard the smallest whisper of his name?

11

It is 2013, and I am in my first year of university. I spend a lot of time with Caleb, a friend from high school who, like me, has ventured into the northern suburbs in a bid to be among it all. He is based at Ormond College and speaks liberally of its trail of antics, of all of the spots on campus that you are meant to have sex in, or on, be it nestled in a bush behind the tennis courts or—if you're game—in some dusty corner of the chapel. It all sounds so intoxicating, so heady and big. One evening, I join him and a group of college friends at a pub close to Ormond for pints. It is a university pub, where students and tutors gather frequently. We are seated inside, and at the bar behind us, an older, respectable-looking gentleman is drinking alone. He is dressed in neat slacks and seems content in his own company. I don't notice him at first. But in due time I am forced to, when a young woman approaches him, taps him on the shoulder and pours a full schooner over his head. The pub falls eerily silent as she stands before him. He is trapped, then, in her line-of-sight. A man made to drip and stink. Eerier again is how he refuses to react. He just sits there as the crisp drizzle of ale dampens his dress shirt and sips at his beer casually. She, bewildered, darts out of the pub. Ten minutes later, he orders another. She is so young. I do not stay long enough to entertain the rumours, to afford the events an appropriate diagnosis. I do find out that he is important, affiliated in some way with Ormond College. Why had she felt compelled to take this man down a peg? From where I stand now, my mind goes mad with speculation. I feel trapped in the wake of many a woman's ruin. They form new dot-points in this memory. I am less haunted by this young woman's gesture to throw a drink than I am with how apt the old man was in ignoring it.

Without institutional backing, women will find their own ways to defy, to rage against something as hard as iron. Isn't it so tempting? To reduce a man to the tremendous weight of embarrassment? There is something so fallible, so animal, about being humiliated. Here, a young woman may want to remind him of this, that he is not a god. I wonder at what point in the timeline of her complaint this woman decided it right to pour a beer over this man's head. How presumptuous of me, to assume her slighted, inveighed against. But why else would one tip the contents of her drink over another person? I want to know what side of the bed she woke that morning. Anger can make for a mighty splint. It can be the brace one needs to mend a broken heart—or worse, a broken spirit. Anger is what Rose has. Blaine as well. Elsie, too, who admits to wanting Harrison's head.

For Cara, it is different. 'I have never felt held by anger,' she tells me during one of our phone conversations. I knew, in deciding to include Cara in this book, that I would find myself challenged by her. When she tells me that she believes Ivan has returned to her, all these years later, due to nursing some presumed break-up, she insists that this is okay with her.

That she doesn't mind. The charge of their sealed love can be found in what is withheld. If she is his craving, the tasty morsel of attention he wants from an arm's length, that makes two of them. She admits to not knowing much about Ivan, that he is—and remains—an idea to her, a fable. Is it so wrong for her to exist in his mind in much the same way? An idea? Is the teacher's fantasy ever as cute as the student's?

If Ivan was waiting for some pardoning from Cara, permission to touch, he was never going to get it. She is careful always with her wants. She will not let them muddy her. If she desired him, which she did, she never would've asked him to settle the score of her wishes. She recalls stories of her childhood, of how—if ever she felt swallowed up by some big, inebriating emotion—her mother would call her a *stupid girl,* would refer to her as *bolshie.* She tells me this, straight-faced and unencumbered. With Ivan, she is hardly bolshie. In fact, I can't imagine Cara ever being that way. She is too curious about people to cast anybody as downright bad. Too curious about herself, I think. If she isn't ever requiring an apology, she isn't ever required to make one. Perhaps in some bid to cut through her composure, I offer a hypothetical.

I borrow it from the others, who are maddened by it. I ask her how it would've felt if she'd found out she was one of many students in Ivan's life, if she were part of a small hoard who had fingered through the stacks of books in his balmy room. If his incense stick, the one he prepared for her arrival, was already charred. She takes a moment and admits that sure, there's no doubt she would've felt jealous. Confused. But then, calmly, 'All is fair in love and war.' By this I take her to mean that, in the grip of something, anything, that philanders with wrongness—be it infidelity or a professor's romantic attention—she can't afford judgement, nor does she care for it. Not long ago, she asked Ivan to tell her something about him. She said to him, 'I forget that you're human' before he answered. Here was a man who existed only in the desert of her lust. He was sans a body and sans—in turn—whatever leaks out of one. No harm, no foul.

*

'I want to be somebody you escape to, not from,' Blaine tells Greg in 2015. By this stage, they have slept together a handful of times, and since then, she has noticed a shift in him. She becomes suspicious that the idea of her is more compelling to him than the real, carnal person she is. Naturally distressed, she requests clarity. 'Has something changed?' she asks him. In this same message she asks if he could just advise her on how to feel about what she has perceived in him as detachment, aloofness. If he tells her that her anxieties are made up, that she is to expect nothing of him, then so be it. She will believe him. Lately she has begun inviting him into the truth of her body's misfortunes, of which there are many. Sometimes she will awake in a cold sweat, gutted by a ferocious cramp. Her back will ache, and her pelvis will wail from its skin casing, and she will require Lori to drag her to the doctor or the emergency room. She does not know then that she has endometriosis, a diagnosis that will take her years to acquire. This, Greg does not care for. She chronicles her hospital stays, her spasms and aches, and he grows bored, responds indifferently. The precocious young student in his mind does not bleed or cry or sting. That person is only there when he wants her to be, when he requires his ego stroked.

As a child, Blaine spent many days and nights admitted at her local public hospital with a gamut of medical issues. She has an autoimmune disease, which took aeons to identify. Her mother, frustrated, would often complain to specialists about how difficult Blaine was, how she never seemed to recover. Her father would visit her almost every day when she was in hospital, and the two would complete quizzes from softcover newsagency game books in warm silence. The job of a good parent is to remedy a child's needs, to wipe them clean of their mess. To be a child, after all, is to require training wheels as one dodders over the honest snags of life. To parent is to omit, to store away a catalogue of lessons and learnings, until the time is right. The job of a good teacher, too. It is not meant to be mucky or earned. But Greg had, in deciding to nuzzle into Blaine's body, made her flesh and bones his business. When he offers her a kiss on that warm night in 2015, he does not realise he has piggybacked a big, treacherous year for her, one that involved a suicide attempt and four long months in a psychiatric facility. I wonder, in speaking to Cara, if she would've become less an idea to Ivan—something real instead—if ever he had reached for her lips. If he had thought to familiarise himself with her birthmarks, her scars and the soft beneath of her underwear. But in hearing of Greg's nonchalance, in how brusquely he divorced himself of Blaine's corporeal needs, I see it possible to remain an idea to someone even still. She feels her body an abattoir of obstacles, resents how it oozes and coughs and makes obvious its decrees. What's worse is so does he.

Some six years later, as a colleague of Greg's and no longer his subordinate, Blaine begins experiencing distressing neurological symptoms. Terrified one evening that she is having an aneurysm, James rushes her to the hospital where she remains for over a year, undergoing every imaginable, invasive test. She discovers she has an incurable inner-ear disorder, which is responsible for her vertigo and chronic migraines. It takes her a long time to return to work or any semblance of normalcy. When she does, she receives a message—out of the blue—from Greg. She apologises to him for having disappeared for some time, explaining the sweep of her ailments. She does this but withholds bits, like how it felt to have a hole chiselled into her skull, to have a doctor probe about her brain and staple her head back together, as if to return her to herself as the stitched-up remains of who she was before this. Greg is as curt as ever in his response. He offers her nothing: no questions, no sympathies, no care. He says, 'You seem fine now,' and it is like a grim yank, a slap in the face.

Hot students don't require attention in the way a lover does. They know how to worship, how to chant in a language they have been taught, how to pet at the wisdom their professor imparts. I am dubious that Greg ever fell in big, proper love with Blaine, as I'm not sure he ever allowed himself to know her. Why would he? She was a prized part of his munificent contract, the perks of a job that afforded him a captive audience. When tutors who procure relationships with their students, even the ones they end up marrying, discuss their origin story—the meet-cute of it all—they often make it out as if they, themselves, were seduced. *And hey, she seduced me!* They'll laugh as if it a fanciful notion, as if they—unlike the seediest of the bunch—are better, less desirous, than the geezers who make it their mission to sleep with their students. Some of them even believe this. Greg tells Blaine, when she queries his fancy for her, that there had been others. But that they had lured him in, had ensnared him with their patient, coquettish eyes. The professor admits that he, unlike her, has a body worth listening to. He does not leave it behind, does not need to. He carts it along to every lecture and notices how it throbs if one such precocious student gets a nice haircut or wears a summer dress he quite likes. That's when his zipper gnaws to be unbarred. His body bespeaks its ugly truth, and he does not care to tune it out.

*

When Elsie's father becomes terminally ill, he regresses. As is the nature of any such ailment, cancer makes him childlike, turns him into a person who needs. She is there to cook for him. To fetch him cigarettes. One afternoon, she undresses him carefully, folding his threads and placing them by the bathroom door to prepare him for a shower. She notices the water stream over her father's tired, naked body, but also doesn't, for she is here as his aid. Care such as this hones our vision. It tells us when, or if, to flinch. This same man taught Elsie how to walk, to put one small foot in front of the other.

Sickness makes humble its servants. It makes once strong, sturdy muscles weak and turns parents into newborns. He writhes in pain well into the evening, and Elsie—unable to sleep and knowing that, in order to do her job properly, she needs rest—puts her headphones in to drown out the noise. How awful it feels, to gum up her father's ache. To have no choice not to. Elsie is a woman who knows the kind of love that disobeys the natural order of things. I ask her one evening what her father would say about her relationship with Harrison, if he were alive. 'There would be no relationship with Harrison if he were alive,' she responds. Yes, because in the grimy tracks of her father's death lives the birth of something else she is to carry: the mastery of a kind of love many of us don't meet until well into our later lives. A love that defies convention. Is it any surprise that Harrison, this older man, with his razor-sharp wit and big, adult needs, proved so alluring?

*

Rose and Ellen, now curled up in the cruel hug of a complaints process, are lucky to have one another. But their remonstrance makes their bodies weak. They want to be heard so badly it begins to hurt. Rose's heart starts to flutter from the stress of it all. A decade earlier, while on a dragged-out hike, she felt it for the first time, and it terrified her. A heart palpitation. It felt as if her big ticker momentarily forgot how to do just that and sank instead into the carpet of her chest. She took a seat and pressed her palm into the centre of her torso, waiting. Her heart quivered about, and she was weakened because of it. Then it clinked back. She had forgotten it for years, that awful sensation. But in the last twelve months, it has returned. She is twenty-eight years old and scared. Adrenaline surges through her from the moment she wakes up. It makes sleeping an unattainable task. She ticks, and ticks some more, and wants to whittle her jaded heart from its cage every time it happens and offer it up to Safer Communities as evidence. 'Look what the bastard is doing to me,' she wants to scream. But he is far away, protected. Every time she imagines him kissing the swollen belly of his student-girlfriend, her chest tightens. If her testimony isn't enough, surely the blaze of her faulty body is. To wither in the dawn of the rest of his life—the birth of his first child—is to feel as if she is crossing a great, dishonourable divide, is a thing contaminated with some recklessness, a badness nobody is willing to name. The only thing worse than a broken heart is a heart strained by something terribly broken.

Ellen, too. In a bid to make manageable her anger, she takes up running. A door will close in her face, and an email will collect dust in some lecturer's inbox, and she will run. She doesn't care to warm up or stretch. She just pelts her legs into the hard terrain. One such run will result in a torn meniscus. In a lot of ways, an injury is how a body complains. Her knee will brim with pain. Will insist she take the weight off of it, that she rest. An institutional complaints process does not gush in as obvious a language. There is no time, and yet ample time, to rest. Time, a necessity when it comes to any reparative gesture, does not exist here. These two women are made static and timeless the moment they lodge a complaint. They are filed away in some far-flung cabinet and put on wicked ice. The world around them carries on, particularly Samuel's world. As far as they are aware, he is still teaching. Occasionally a paper of his will be published in some creditable academic journal, and they will sieve through it for clues, for some proof that he has felt the brunt of their efforts. He is so untouchable, and they instead are so touched, so tampered with, so tired.

One evening, three months into the complaints process, Rose gets drinks with Mel, a close friend of hers. Mel is a fierce socialist, who bumps into another friend from organising named Ted at the pub. Mel likes Ted, but—having since ended a relationship of four years with a man named Darcy, someone high up in socialist organising who perpetuated a range of sexist exploits towards her and many others—she has grown suspicious of Ted's maintenance of that friendship with him. Aware of this, Rose badgers Ted over drinks. She won't let him get away with it. She squeezes her fists together and speaks with a snake-laced temper when Ted defends his stance. She hates the way he draws in air when he speaks, as if sucking it. How he refuses to look her in the eye. Perhaps this frustration is borrowed from her own dalliance with a complaints process, with Samuel, but she's too far gone. Her body surges with routine adrenaline.

To cool off, Ted suggests the three of them take a breath and head back to his apartment, which is a stone's throw from the pub. He has ketamine and cocaine and the promise of robust conversation. *What the heck*, Rose thinks. The three mosey down, make themselves comfortable among his purring cats, and Rose—cocky and eager—snorts two big lines of each bag in quick succession. She is buzzing. Eventually, though, something happens. She feels her heart retire into her ribcage and her eyes begin to flutter. Her body melts into the couch atop of Mel's, who—stressed—decides to call the paramedics. 'It's my friend. Her lips are blue,' she hears Mel attesting, but she can't move. Rose's legs seize up, and all of the colour from her face drains into the sofa beneath her. She tries to scream but can't open her mouth. She hears someone, who sounds and pleads just like her, howling. But she can't be sure that the racket is hers. She knows Mel is crying and Ted is terrified. Later, she finds out that while she was atrophied on his couch, he was on the phone to his mother. Alone in the yawning quiet of her mind, it's as if she presses her ear against the thin walls of her brain and waits for a sign. Mel wipes the drool from the pillow and holds Rose's head in her chest instead. Rose, now still, pleads with her body to forgive her, to let her come back. She wants to be who she was before this. By this, she means all of this. A lone inch between life and death, between good and bad. A weak heart, made weaker by her burly spirit.

When Rose eventually tells me about what happened that night, she laughs, tapering her flirtation with death so as to make it seem a strange, hollow mishap. 'I'm happy to be here,' she says, briefly sincere. 'I have so much work to do.'

12

When I first begin corresponding with Blaine, she promises to offer up her university's integrity module for me to look at. It is a unit of study aptly titled 'Appropriate Workplace Behaviour' that all faculty are expected to complete if they are to teach. She is thirty-nine years old when she does and is struck while working through it by how often university policy is disregarded by staff. In each dot point, she unearths Greg's dogged pursuit of her when she was in her twenties. In each anecdote, a younger, more wide-eyed version of herself is made a shadow puppet for all the workforce to see. She becomes the gauge for whether or not harm was done, without the knowledge of her colleagues. Blaine considers it almost upsetting how easy it is to just skip through each question, how outlandishly specific—and yet enormously vague—each sketch of a power imbalance is. 'No "type" of power is inherently good or bad', the module spells out. 'It is critical that our staff are conscious of power dynamics in the workplace and actively consider how their use of different power types can positively or negatively impact others.'

I want to rinse my curiosities of bias, of judgement. I want to understand the kind of professor who makes a lover out of his students. I want to know whether or not he ever found himself confused about its wrongness, if he were ever taught to question his wants. Is this too generous a tail to chase? Too kind a theory? Is power blinding, in that a man can crawl into its lap and forget that it has, in due time, brandished him more invincible than before? Or do these men see hopeful, puffed-up boys with bones to pick and bills to pay when they consider the sort of people they are, eager only for a pretty girl to like them?

Even if we are to imagine a tutor ignorant to his influence, is this grounds to assume him blameless? If he is to pursue a relationship with a student, be it former or current, and that relationship is to end up rotten and splintered years later, is it still wrong if he never considered his conduct as such? I have come to learn that these instances of sexual misconduct differ significantly from cases of sexual assault or even harassment. They lack a vein of suspicion that haunts many arenas of sexual violence. If a woman is raped, she is often disbelieved, burdened with the need to prove it. But women, like the ones I am speaking to, do not necessarily rub up against this same kind of doubt as sexual assault survivors when it comes to declaring having once been loved by their superiors. This love? *Yes, it happened.* The woman who signs a lease with her professor is believed, is known to have been held and kissed and coddled by him. She is instead encumbered with the task of proving that, in those gestures, lived a kind of wrongness. 'Yes, it happened. Yes, how many times must I remind you that I know this? That I know it happened! Yes, I was there. It happened, but it shouldn't have. Yes, I loved him. But I never should've been made to.'

I have spoken to many women throughout writing this book. Lots have divulged scattered, nugatory memories to me. I've heard about tutors who—in the dead of night—emailed them links to Bandcamp mixtapes they themselves made, warbling songs laced with innuendo. And others whose professors started following them on Instagram and who left love-heart-eyed emojis—or worse, fire emojis—on their selfies. Some who accept invitations to undergraduate parties, only to slur some wearisome sentence as they help themselves to the esky, insisting that, 'Tonight, I am not your tutor. I am just me.'

There was the man who, over dinner, told his student that his colleagues would no doubt be jealous. That they all wanted her as well. These are hardened truths, hardly able to be contested. But are they injudicious? For every such drifting wrongdoing is another person who insists that their parents, who met this way, are happily married. I watch an Instagram reel, on repeat, of a woman sipping wine with her fiancé on a terrace balcony in Greece, paired with a caption that reads, 'Once upon a time, you were just strangers who got close while working on a philosophy assignment. Now you're engaged on a balcony in Greece.' She had responded to one of my many callouts earlier in the year, avowing that she and her partner had met in the classroom while he was her tutor. She referred to herself as lucky. A friend of hers leaves a comment on her reel that reads, 'Philosophy! You two are so cute', to which she responds cutely, 'We are a cliché, I'm sorry.' Ironically, here is a woman determined to prove the absence of wrongness. A binary catches fire on whatever side of the fence a relationship such as this fall upon.

When Elsie's Safer Communities officer suggests she go to the police instead, she laughs. 'The police?' she tells me, exasperated. 'Why would I go to the police when nothing criminal happened?' I, like her, find it an offensive suggestion. It implies a preposterousness to her complaint, that she is—if anything—hysterical. What are the police to do? Arrive stoney-faced and browbeat at the classroom of her tutor? Cuff him? Pedagogical relationships are grey and intricate. At worst, the harms are material: a bitter work environment, a shrinking academic reference. At best (or worst again, in differing ways), the harms are symbolic: a tarnished sense of self; the vinegary taste of indignity; a cold nudge that one is, above all else, forever gendered. Or something else entirely, of which I am trying to pin.

An integrity module can warn staff of the trauma that can arise when it comes to breaching professional lines, but it can't—or won't—name that same trauma. I grow bored of searching for intelligent articles and books on the topic. I am to sift through a gamut of erotica when I do, to make something out of the titillating charge that lives in the taboo of it all. For every essay on sexual misconduct are five XXX films of a woman in red-framed glasses, whose breasts jostle out from her crisp white dress shirt as she sits atop a desk before a chalkboard. It is all so monotonous, so crude. What am I to do with all this?

Is it that these women are all adults? Is that what makes this tricky? Do we wake, on the dawn of our ascent into maturity, and feel rickety and changed? I am a tattoo artist. I notice how teenagers arrive at my studio door, hissing with excitement. They will often come accompanied by a small hoard of friends, each with freshly pierced noses and winged eyeliner meticulously applied, each gossiping about some spry dilemma. They are so young. I shave each of their arms with care. I am aware that, while gripping my needle, I can make or break the skin of some child, if I want to. Instead,

I dab gently on the bloody lines of my work, wrap their arms in cling wrap, and wish them well. I do not take.

*

I sense in Elsie an unease when it comes to bringing such a shadowed thing to the surface. Is she to rehome this mess? To offer it up to a coop as official, as sanctioned, as a formal complaints process? Is this where it is to live now? In embarking on a secret relationship, one inhabits a new set of rules. I sense this too in Rose, but it is different. Rose was never untold. With Samuel, she was his unconcealed pride and joy, an out-and-proud exception to the rule. Samuel's own father had married a former student, long before meeting Samuel's mother. This made Rose lore, of both the institutional and familial kind. When Josephine encourages Rose to keep her knowledge of the complaints process, largely through Ellen, to herself, she scoffs. 'When did this all become so hush-hush?' she thinks. Perhaps this feeling is not unique. I imagine anyone made begrimed by some wrongdoing to find its ceremonial unearthing bitter and comical. Rose does not want to be bound by such good behaviour in the shadow of such bad. She finds the pleasantries she is expected to uphold so short-sighted, so unfair. If a professor can make unaccounted-for love to his student, why can't his student—now slighted and resentful—make unaccounted-for hate to him?

*

Jade, a friend of mine who is a tutor herself, speaks to me often about how absent any kind of training is when it comes to teaching university classes. I am curious as to what sort of training would, or could, prevent sexual misconduct in tertiary education. I find it comforting to imagine a stern, hands-on approach. I indulge in fantasy for a brief moment and in my mind's eye see a strident senior female academic, with broad hips and a burning gaze, strolling assuredly before a classroom display of male professors. She takes her time with them. 'So,' she begins. 'You want to fuck your students, hey?' One such geezer shuffles uncomfortably in his chair, and she notices this, makes a concerted effort to badger him during her tirade, will slap him silly with printouts of feminist texts.

On X, I stumble across a video of ten or so female students pressing posters up against a set of glass doors in protest. The caption reads, '2 UT professors were found guilty of sexual misconduct. They are still allowed to teach. The university has taken bandaid measures on the issue and continues to put students in danger through their inaction.' The women are chanting furiously as they conduct a student-led sit-in. I see in their objection a gesture to teach. Without sufficient training from official channels, the burden of remedying the issue of sexual misconduct falls squarely on the shoulders of those most affected.

The script that makes it permissible for a professor to pine for his attractive, precocious female student, even to sleep with her, is hardened and tedious. It is a patriarchal legacy, a rite of passage. I consider here *Lolita*, the renowned, albeit controversial, classic from Vladimir Nabokov. As a teenager, I myself had a printed-out poster of its cover stuck to my wall.

While writing this, I notice on my bookshelf an old copy of *Lolita*, a book that revels in the apparent joys and aches of hebephilia. It is frayed and damaged. Over the years, I have cut snippets from its cover to occasionally make roaches for joints. There is something so hackneyed about a man who pines for a woman under his heel, and in the lecture hall, this pulse can be satisfied. It can be made safe and shiny with significantly less problematic age parameters. I do not doubt that there are impressive, loveable students who jolt their teachers out of some monotonous slumber. That among the student body, there are well-versed postgraduates who inspire their supervisors. Whether or not this delight ought to be the stuff of sex is where I become less enchanted. Why is the professor who insists his student-girlfriend is clever beyond her tutelage, who endeavours to cushion his desire for her in legitimacy, who decides her his equal, not the same man who dates female professors instead? If what he claims to be attracted to is intelligence, if his want for it spills out and only onto certain students, why not look elsewhere—in his department, perhaps—where he is more likely to find it? The hebephile is attracted to children on the brink of puberty, who are making sense of its cruel promise as it cuts through their youth. The professor who yearns for his student is different, obviously.

But still, I sense in him a pull towards something emerging and imminent, to the sparkle of a young woman's potential as she sees, in him, a world she hopes for herself.

To Blaine, Greg will admit to having shared his poetry with Jenna. Fed up with the pageantry of it all, Blaine, frustrated, tells him off. Taken aback, Greg will insist that he is merely conversing with a fellow writer, a woman attentive to and intrigued by similar things. This is how he bargains Jenna's adulthood, how he makes it work for him. She is not a child, after all. And he is just making friends. Having taught Jenna herself, Blaine is dubious. Yes, Jenna was an unwavering kind of student, always captivated by the work. But it's not as if she was exceptionally good or talented. She wasn't well-placed to challenge or stimulate Greg, apart from, of course, being twenty-five years old and having a cute, strawberry-blonde fringe that bounced when she laughed. 'He said I was cruel,' Blaine scoffs. He forgets, while being schooled by Blaine, his protégé, how tangible the galaxy of his desires remain to her even still. He fails to remember how the two would sit, huddled on the furthermost part of his marital bed, and listen to iPhone recordings of his guitar solos just because.

I ask Blaine what sort of institutional training could prevent cases of sexual misconduct such as hers. 'That is a question I have no answer for, especially when an educator is bringing personal baggage into the classroom,' she tells me.

I recall, the year I met my once-upon-a-time tutor, how I'd jotted him down in my diary. I was besotted at the time, and—like a schoolgirl with a crush—made a list of all the things I knew and liked about him: the outfits he'd wear, catchphrases he'd recite, details of his personal life he readily offered up to his class. When I tell Jade this, how he willed into existence his life outside of the classroom, she sneers. This she tends to avoid. What good does it do, imagining your tutor heartbroken, or enraptured in some crowd at a gig, or tired? Elsie tells me how Harrison too would offer up nuggets of his personal life in his tutorials, would slowly blight any boundary lines between his students and himself. She describes how, before they began sleeping together, if he happened to bump into her at university or saw her in some corridor, the two would lock eyes and warmly begin to laugh. If I am to scrutinise these interactions, I find it almost unsavoury imagining the man brought to a halt in her presence and thinking to giggle. 'It's you. There you are,' is what he says to her with his dimples all those times, when he shares with Elsie the lingering of some small, cherished interval. 'It's you, and it's me. It's us.' To cultivate this, a thing deliberately small. An intimacy so slight, so considered, it makes for the construction of some inside language, a way of speaking directly to her—through her?—through the hush of his body, the fullness of his smile. 'I see you,' he says in all of the words he chooses not to use, knowing full well how keen she is to hear it.

13

PORN OFTEN RENDERS TIME useless. When I say this, I don't mean for it to come across as a judgement. But, as I sleuth through Pornhub's archives after having plugged 'professor student' into its search engine, I notice how unsparing the titles of its films are, how obvious porn delegates itself to a lone task: to make somebody cum. In this sense, porn concedes to a moment and does its best to decide for its viewer when, or how, that moment ought to arise. 'Here, when the woman croaks a little, is when you give way to climax,' it may insist. 'If that doesn't work, 0.37 seconds later ought to do it, when her face is caked with wetness.' There are no panoramas in porn, no unbroken views. At least not in the porn I am researching for this book. There are, instead, titles like *Teen Sluts that Fuck in Detention*, or *Pigtailed Students Who Suck Cock in Classroom*, or *Skinny Teens Who Get Good Grades the Easy Way*. Each blur of body and tunic begin to seep into the other, and it is late, so I close the tabs and stare despondently at my screen, unsure how best to make sense of it all. In these fleeting clips that trifle only with climax, a singular, fixed story is being told.

What strikes me about all of the women's stories I am collecting is how they cannot be contained. They are made up not of singular moments, but a wide, sweeping brush of disorderliness. The impacts of their relationships with their tutors and professors make for lives chiselled by strange, eternal wounds, an ache they are eager to treat or at least to understand.

On Pornhub, a *Schoolgirl Shows Professor How Much She Cares About Education*, and manages to do so in ten tidy minutes. In real life, Elsie drafts a letter to her university that synoptically explains her plight, only to edit it tirelessly. She will open the document four days in a row before letting it rot in her laptop. For her, it has been three years. A *Teen Slut Earns an A After Class* in seven minutes, and Rose makes a meme describing Samuel's indiscretions in three minutes, labels it a little 'red hot' and sends it to me, paired with a laughing emoji. It has been nine years since they first met. In twelve heady minutes, a porn star *Agrees To Help Her Professor & They Get Turned On*, and Blaine decides it best she mute Greg's social media updates so as not to have her day ruined with his self-absorbed reminders. It has been eight years since he touched her, and fifteen since he unsnarled some complex language equation on his whiteboard for her to understand. For Cara, the moment never comes. She makes a collage out of Ivan's words but is careful not to stick too many of his idioms atop of one another, to avoid collision. Without any obvious crescendo, she is left alone to her devices, can even—if she wishes—employ Ivan as one of those devices himself. It suits them both.

Rose is mortified when she admits to having masturbated, in the spire of her anger, to the notion of being ignored in Samuel's classroom. What strikes me about the scene she describes is how truant any wail of sex is in her retelling.

There are no unclad bodies, no glaring thrusts. Nobody cums, and nobody leaves. The spectacle is, in a lot of ways, sexless. It differs from all of the places my mind wanders if I'm alone and restless. It reeks instead of a searing need to place some shoddy feeling, the presence of something staggering and leaky that lives in Rose. Without any kind of institutional purging, her body will decide instead where to place her frustration, will plot out its climax. It is all so humiliating, so cruel. And yet this is how she gets off. This is how she makes it hers.

The first time Rose and Samuel have sex, he is shy. He does not remove his underwear. She instead is naked. The sex itself is gentle and gracious, and for many clean months, Rose will feel fixed by him—as if with him she can leave all of the bullshit of her adolescence behind, can be loved. While she had only slept with a few men before him, she was already jaded. One such boyfriend had insisted she let him aggressively 'finger-bang' her while she lay motionless in his single bed. It hurt a lot, but he had pulled up a video for reference he had found online, of a porn star whimpering in presumed pleasure while four big men each placed their fingers into her, one by one, as if she a cadaver worth exploring. This, he said, is what he wanted. And Rose, at eighteen years old, wanted nothing more than to be just that: wanted, in the eyes of some boy. Then there was someone with longish, blond hair who she had met in one particular class at university. They went on a small handful of dates, and he lived with his parents in a well-off area in Melbourne's south. The house was undergoing renovations, and she remembers being seated atop of the wooden chassis of some refurbished skeleton of a room while he pleaded she let him sleep with her. His prayers echoed, due to there being no roof, no walls. It took him nearly three hours, but—inevitably—she agreed. During the act itself, he accidentally referred to her as his sister's name, and she cowered in embarrassment.

The shame Rose feels about how she has abstracted her hurt and mangled it sexy is obvious. What is more obvious is the lack of shame present in the male professors, how hollow their wants are. I feel around in the darkness of their burning needs and find no semblance of abashment. Greg, in 2015, sends Blaine a message, declaring that a photograph she had attached in one of their messages of a bruise on her leg was suggestive. 'Maybe you weren't aware,' he prefaces. Then the married man leaves comments on photo-booth shots of her and her cat, pointing out the cuteness of her pussy. The first time they sleep together, he asks if he can cum inside her. He returns her squarely into the domain of sex. He makes crude their interactions and does so again. Perhaps this is how Rose arrived at the place she did, during the first week of her finding out about Sienna. In Samuel's new relationship lives a rough-hewn truth about her: that she is sex above all else. The fantasy she imagines is one where he brushes her aside while she is seated in his classroom once more. In it, she notices him enjoy the presence of some slimmer, younger student, and it is a truth too nasty to make good, honest sense of. If Samuel is to make his students sex, sex is what she will become. She may as well enjoy it.

*

The first man Blaine ever falls in love with is someone she never meets in person. Instead, they get to know each other online, having met on ICQ, a cross-platform instant messaging website. His name is Amaro, and he is American. He drinks Heineken out of paper cups in front of the television every time the Dallas Cowboys itch towards a win. He dresses himself in Tommy Hilfiger and often has the cinnamon tang of Wrigley's Big Red chewing gum on his tongue between meals at Applebee's. Amaro is cartoonish in how much of a Yankee he appears to Blaine, who—at barely fifteen years old—has struck up a mystifying bond with him, a man just shy of twenty-eight. For years, they chat almost daily. Then they delegate their conversations to emails and parcels. The two send each other photographs and letters in the mail, and Blaine—incredibly lonely—takes gusto in how regularly and adamantly they converse with one another. She hates school then and finds ways to writhe her way out of catching the school bus, eager to miss a day or two. ICQ is how she establishes closeness, even with people in her own town, fellow students with whom she forges meaningful connections without the awkwardness of standing before them face-to-face.

Both she and Amaro never intend to meet. A year into their exchanges, he—quite appalled with himself—mentions to her, 'I think I am love with a sixteen-year-old girl.' She doesn't necessarily believe she is in love with him, but she does love him dearly. He is something of a saving grace, a salve. With Amaro, her body is not a thing she needs to grimace at. Attention not something she feels she ought to beg for. Amaro is complex, and his big, tumultuous life is gripping. He knows the sound and celerity of sirens, had run to Canada to leave a DUI charge behind. There had been police on his tail who had been designated to make his arrest. He begins referring to himself by another name. He has a child. But with Amaro, Blaine is not sex. She is something else entirely, something cerebral. Their shared intrigue is an experiment on how to muse, how to brood over each other's worlds—and words—and this, she likes. In him, she hears a man eager to hurtle from the rugged upset of adulthood. She, on the other hand, finds adolescence quite dreadful, thinks it makes for a lonesome trip. They meet in the middle. In this online rink, time is also rendered useless. Blaine is awake and tying the laces of her school shoes while Amaro sleeps. Amaro stirs and propels himself sluggishly into the inertness of his day while Blaine rests. 'Yes,' she tells me. 'It may have been an inappropriate relationship for a man to have had with a teenager. But he was my friend and confidant.'

When Blaine turns seventeen, Amaro contracts AIDS. Unable to pay for health insurance and determined not to die a slow, belittling death, he raises a deer rifle to his head and pulls the trigger. When Blaine first tells me this, I shriek in shock. It isn't until I sit with it a moment longer, when I let the jadedness of my research sour my view, that I consider him a fraud. I imagine that Blaine is—to him—nothing more than some ball he can piff over the fence of his faraway fancy, and chase. That perhaps this man, with his labyrinth of painful stories, has played a cruel hoax on a teenage girl, a child who hangs off of his every word. He may have even grown bored of her. May have fallen in love with somebody else, who had stumbled across Blaine's letter and photographs and who rightly found his flirtations with a girl as young as her so off-putting. Did he stage his own demise?

But days before his suicide, Blaine receives a goodbye letter in the mail. As is the nature of such a large stretch of ocean, she will only receive it once he is gone. 'If my house were burning down, I'd grab the cats and that letter,' she reflects. Given Blaine is able to access his death notice online, as well as his funeral arrangements, I am proven wrong about Amaro. Blaine grieves him, a friend she imagines as having been proud of her, thrilled for where she has ended up if he were here to see it. If anything, their love materialises as paternal. In the wake of Amaro's suicide, Blaine is left with a small tenderness: that of being made special, of being one of the last people a man, in the chokehold of a grizzly fall from grace, thought of.

In Blaine's hankering for a kind of love devoid of touch, I see instead a girl made whole. Made sans a body and all of the baggage that comes with it. In her teenage years, she did not want to leak and smell and change. Cared not for a period, so when her child body thought to do as child bodies do and exchanged the meat on its bones for small, aching breasts and yawning hips, she hated it. She arrives at the gates of her university years later, ready—and eager—to rack her brain. Here, Greg's gesture to sleep with her is to introduce sex into a place meant to be sexless. Formative, yes. Sacred, most definitely. Here, he decides not to care. To close his eyes to how often, and how readily, women are made sex in the first place.

I have long stumbled upon the tireless work of women who are made frazzled and torn when they try to divorce themselves from their bodies. Women who yearn to be taken seriously. These professors, for all their expertise, remain unable to buck the blinding impulse to twiddle about where they shouldn't. Instead, they will lodge their well-oiled boot in the doorframe of a woman's education, her relationship to herself, and keep it there. This is how Rose's mind wanders. Samuel has wedged his dull foot between the classroom and the bedroom, and Rose—baffled—does not know what to do with his interference, nor what side of the hatch she is expected to live in now. So the two rooms become muddled, and once she eventually bites the courage to slam the door, to have it quake in its hinges, it is only her whose fingers are left in its egress, made sandwiched and bruised. These same fingers, the ones that will have her topple over into climax. Still, she'll want to wash them, again and again.

*

What if they were just to look? To cast their eyes on the young scholars before them and not make damp their gaze? What if it were that simple? I message Jade while scouring through Pornhub's archive of professor–student porn. 'Fucking hell,' I snigger, pleading she join me in my stunt. Almost immediately, Jade will notice how women roll into frame, their mouths agape like tidy, wet inlets. Sometimes the shot will find itself fixed only to her body, and the professor instead will be faceless, made discernible with each occasional grunt or the outline of an erection. He is heard, but she is seen. His pleasure pulsates, and she—on the other hand—clenches her palms, or mouth, or hips around it, makes do it with as she ought to. When she looks at him, what does she see? I am distracted by this. It is as if, in these short, homespun clips, some truth materialises. How habitually women are gaped at, and how ceaselessly men can remain lofty, untouched. It is easy then to imagine a professor, not equipped with some terrible lifetime chronicle of being ogled at, finding joy in the wanton gaze of his students. Attention is attention, after all. The lecture hall becomes his stage, where he is to cavort about and perform something of a mating dance, can hop aboard the legacy of long-dead scholars and make it his. It doesn't bother him if he is an idea to some shiny young thing, if she sees Proust, or Marx, or Sartre when she looks. In this way, she projects onto the man something transcendent, spots in him an obvious brilliance. But when he casts his eyes on her, he sees, at worst, a plaything. At best, a muse.

When Cara is a teenager, her mother will take up photography. This will be one of many of her creative pursuits, and to Cara she is unrivalled in how she approaches various crafts. Cara's mother is the kind of woman who, when she puts her mind to something, makes it hers. She poses her children on varying stoops. Has them peer curiously towards her lens and envelops them in assorted styles of lighting, to make for good studio practice. Cara, as well as her sister, have their faces become ablaze with citrus light or a cool, misty wash, depending on the mood their mother is eager to evoke. It is all quite lovely, being looked at this way. Her mother finds the pronunciation of her craft in the soft weld of Cara's cheeks. But in becoming her mother's subject, Cara notices her appearance being inspected. She smiles, and her mother professes it a strange, unpleasant smile. Cara is too gaping with it. It makes for an expression too gaudy and big, so her mother suggests she do it better. 'Smile with your eyes,' she tells Cara. Mothers, often unaware, will reveal to their daughters a glossary of insecurities, of things to fix. They make their observations known, whether zipping up a dress and noticing it has become tight, or brushing out a child's braids and discovering a hoard of split ends. In the dawn of her mother's feedback, Cara learns the value of making her smile demure. She is not to be over-the-top and must not grin like an idiot. She keeps her emotional expressions buried in the recesses of what once was. Knows not to let on. It is too treacherous otherwise. As a child, she had long found her smile a little embarrassing. She had hoped to hide her gums from the rest of the world. She learns, while sitting atop some stool in her mother's workshop, how she can have the best of both worlds. Can make a servant out of her insecurities and show her teeth all the same. No-one ought to know the rest of it. It being the stuff of hidden joy. Her gummy parts.

14

During our correspondence, Blaine will often message me while wending her way through her university's gardens. Come spring, the jacarandas bloom, creating a lavender canopy across various lawns and pathways. It is a lavish architectural maze, and the flowerets make its beauty all the more obvious, giving it a certain opulence it does not need. There is a marked prestige to each of these institutions, and at various junctures in my research, I find it difficult to bear knowing what I know. I will even step foot in a few of them, just to see. I'm eager to notice their maintenance, how kept the lawns and pristine the halls. While writing this book, I meet Joni on campus, a friend of mine who is completing her PhD at the University of Sydney. I slog through this manuscript in one of its many buildings, a place with floorboards I am eager to peel back to peer beneath. The veneer of it all is so charming, it becomes easy to forget the underbelly of sexual misconduct that exists in Australia's Go8, the number of instances—be it reported or otherwise—that make splintered its big quartz walls, that make hushed its student body.

What is power? And why is it that where there is power, abuse seems almost always prescribed? The gesture to beautify some university ground, to dress it in garishness, is an exercise in preserving reputation. Its beauty makes for reliable cladding. I notice, while sitting on the stairs at the University of Sydney, so many young female students petering in and out of buildings. I hate how suspicious I have become, how convinced I am of the presence of some hideous troll that makes puppets out of its tutors, that spits insults from the grimy lake it sleeps in. I entertain sticking up A4 tear-off printables on the back doors of many leading university bathroom stalls and having my phone number printed onto every small divide, insisting that—if ever a student has slept with their professor—they reach out. If my private messages are anything to rely upon, every prestigious university throbs with a million-and-one affairs. And why do I feel like some kind of anomaly in considering pedagogical relationships so fraught with danger? So equally avoidable? It feels as if each discipline—but largely the humanities—has made it so its student body are to surrender to some stale marriage where the philandering parties carry on, hopeful that, if never caught, there is no need to confess. Have I stumbled across some invisible rite of passage, a long-established varnish whose shine I find cheap and metallic?

Elsie stresses Harrison's respect from the beginning. He is well-liked and charming. Having worked as a tutor at his institution for upwards of fifteen years, he has made many good impressions. One afternoon, while discussing the nature of my research at a party, an acquaintance tells me about her particular university and how rumours had circulated years ago regarding one of the tutors and an alleged relationship he had been in with a student. She didn't want to believe the hearsay, having babysat his son, having relied on him at various periods of her own degree. Very quickly do I discover it is Harrison she is speaking of, and I feel momentarily dragged into Elsie's plight. What I know becomes windswept and susceptible. I consider how awful the battery of making a fuss in some man's colosseum would be. These men are as manicured as the mown grass upon which they play, as decorated as the high ceilings and untarnished theatre halls they engineer their wants in. To square up with them is to square up with the academy as a whole. She stresses that she has no idea who the student is or was, and I feel a momentarily pang of relief.

Wherever there is power, there are pecking orders. There are few establishments as hierarchical in nature as academia. Early on in Elsie's degree, she joins Harrison and a handful of other honours students for a picnic at the Edinburgh Gardens, where they are meeting to discuss the year ahead. Harrison is seated among the hopeful crew, nibbling carelessly on a blade of grass. Here, he states, with cocky nonchalance, that very few of the students seated before him today will become successful painters in their own right. Elsie is unsure how to respond to a claim as demoralising as this. It makes her dreams feel paltry, places her back into her childhood bedroom, a girl with dirtied fingers who completes some hideous paint-by-numbers kit. How has she wound up here, only to be rendered so naive, so hopeless? Having been a bookish high-school student myself, I recall the pang of shame I felt when I received a distinction, a meagre mark of 75, for the first essay I handed in at university. There was a foreboding presence of disparagement in each and every 'crit' I attended at the Victorian College of the Arts. I even remember one of my tutors telling a student that he'd likely end up taking Santa photos at the local mall if he wasn't careful.

Often I will drive past the University of Melbourne's expansive college grounds, with its pale towers and the imposing gates of its colleges. It possesses an air of mystique, as do all sandstone universities. These castles, these magnificent castles. They harbour many a whisper, I'm sure. Many a remedy for how best to deconstruct the systems we take for granted, the ones that determine how the world operates. They throb with promise and exclusivity. Jade, whose father has calloused hands and earns an honest pay cheque in a factory he runs in the outer suburbs, describes to me how untranslatable her academic craft is to him. She tells me how backbreaking it is to recount such obtuse ways of thinking, to offer them up to her family over dinner. This is because her family knows just how backbreaking it isn't. Their bodies labour instead. They ache in all of the decent ways a body ought to. If you aren't invited into the milieu of scholastic prestige, it is impossible to understand it. Perhaps that is the point. Perhaps it always was the point. I understand Jade's plight. When I was enrolled as a student of Fine Arts, my parents found it unfeasible. Frustrating, if anything. Did I really believe I was going to become a famous artist? University was meant to be vocational, they stressed. So I left. The following year, I was accepted to study Arts/Law at Monash University.

One evening, as a flashy nod to being accepted into Monash University's undergraduate cohort of law students, the institution hosted a canapé night, inviting each of us and our parents to mingle. I, a begrudging tyro, invited my father to join me, a man who has long boasted about never having read a book in his life. I watched, amused, as he keenly roved through a sea of attorneys and their smug sons, beer in hand. 'We thought it'd be handy if she became a lawyer,' I heard him recount to more than one geezer. 'That way she can keep us out of jail.' He'd then laugh a little and peer around eagerly, only to find my eyes among the haughty crowd, crack a smile, and rove some more. I laughed alongside him, so as to have it seem a cute inside joke between the two of us.

To be a student, even as an adult, is to find oneself entitled to its many milestones. I am the first person in my family to graduate high school. My mother never signed the breast pocket of some school blouse, her mind made fuzzy with last-day jelly shots while she excitedly gripped her sharpie. My father never folded the sleeves of his blazer before attending some valedictory dinner. There are no framed degrees in my family home, no brooches fastened to lapels. No hinged pins and catches. 'You know, I never attended my graduation,' Rose tells me. When I ask her why, she shrugs. 'It didn't feel important.' What she doesn't tell me is that by the time she finishes her Arts degree, Samuel has relocated. He is teaching at a different institution. They no longer carpool. Without thinking, she reorganises her remaining units so she can complete them online instead. She drags her feet through the surviving modules as if each one a dead weight, a burden she no longer cares to bear. Somewhere along the way, he became her locus of study instead. His love a neater fit than any trencher or gown, more portentous than a ceremony. She fades into the ether of some speculative hoo-ha, is almost embarrassed to not match his rank. So she retires quietly. She doesn't care for any boring formalities, any lousy old fuss. She will crawl into his arms instead.

*

Death is as much a milestone as it is a millstone. It gnaws at Elsie, and she is vigilant to its call, how primed it is to take her father. Eventually, it does.

Death is a modest, ragged nest. It does not announce itself. How scarcely it offers itself up for scheduling and instead decides to creep into the home unannounced, while the rest of life sleeps, and rifle about in the bunk of a good man's sickness. It will decide—with no consultation—it is time. There are no placards or streamers or the promise of a school-funded bar tab. And yet, Elsie is to graduate, is to arrive in the next chapter of her life, with a lump in her throat that takes years to lessen.

Death will mark her. It will break her open some nights. She will leave the pub a handful of weeks later and find herself paralysed, retching over a friend's toilet bowl, having collapsed into a kind of wailing that leaves even the strongest winded. So when Harrison decides—on that fateful day in the gardens, six months later—that she, along with the others, will almost most definitely not make it, she determines it her mission to prove him wrong. There is not much to lose, as it is already lost. She is to earn her stripes, is to make it all count for something. Later, in the warmth of Harrison's bed, he will instead declare her prolific beyond her years. Will even suggest there are options for her to pursue a PhD straight out of Honours, to exhibit her paintings widely. Here, the older man opens many doors, and Elsie—her face and hands still splintered from how death slammed its own door in her presence—will revel in Harrison's promises, will come to him knocking.

*

At various junctures of writing this, the women I'm speaking with will remind me of my own power. Cara will say, while the two of us are seated at an Italian restaurant in Melbourne's CBD, that it is all quite adult how I am working on a second book. Elsie will ask me, in discussions around my sentiments towards the academy, if I'd ever consider returning. Dusting myself off and getting a postgraduate degree. 'Not that you necessarily need to, given the career you've forged,' she will offer politely. In interrogating the murkiness of power, I become suspicious of my own. In these pages, I am authoritative. I'm extractive in my research. There are many women who have hoisted one leg into the grotto of their memories and trimmed a nugget of truth from the flowstone of some forgotten place, offering it up to me. More, whose anecdotes I won't mention, whose chronicles I can't necessarily place. I am to expect so much from my subjects. I strive to offer them the same, deciding to immerse our conversations with my own hapless confessions. But it never seems like enough.

One evening, six months into our conversations, Blaine—while seated in the driver's seat of her car—notices a pool of blood between her legs. I am aware she is eager for children, and she tells me, a week or so prior, that she has discovered she is pregnant. I am elated when she does, in much the same way I am thrilled to hear of the cut and colour of the wedding dress she is to be married in come June the following year. And then, in swift procession, she miscarries. She messages me from the stuffy confines of the emergency department, where she waits for an answer, for help. The stakes feel so high, so real. I am working to a deadline and—in turn—so are they. They will slip into action, will carve time out of their own big lives to aid me. And yet, I am scaffolded in ways they aren't, am made to matter. How does one write to power when one feels her position is made so muscular?

Yes, I have bound these women together. How, in each one having had some kind of relationship with a professor or tutor, I fear I have accidentally hedged them all into the same class. I have decided it the only thing that matters. After all, isn't this entirely what I have come to resent about the gesture to fuck one's student in the first place? How it stains a person, renders them a part of some pattern? And yet, here each of these women are: my own private directory of student-lovers.

I hoped, though, in revealing more of them to my readers—their marvellous, big selves—I'd be able to make their scope obvious and beautiful, to insist they are more complex, more intricate than what was decided for them by their superiors.

I spend a lot of time on each of these professor's websites and social media pages. I study them eagerly while simultaneously not caring to know them, to afford them as much liberty to be whole, in the way I have their students. Yes, if I were to be let in, to appear in the doorframe of each of their homes and ask them to self-diagnose their habits, insist they snake through their lives for me, I'd probably find many an answer. But this, I avoid. Elsie will tell me about Harrison's contempt for his own father, a man who philandered through marriage. Rose will reveal the hex that sprouts in Samuel's family tree, how his own father got hitched to a student from his philosophy class way back when, sometime in the eighties. How mathematical it all seems, how obvious. But in choosing to render these men two-dimensional, I feel I am restoring some corruption that lives in the bricks and mortar of the academy. You see, they aren't meant to be known. Not like this. Neither are their students, but this is what happens. Women, lit up only by flesh and by bones, by heat and spit. I find it all so greedy.

*

It is late 2024, and Rose finds proof online that Samuel has—in the tenth month of having had a complaint filed against him—been offered a prestigious grant. He is to write a monograph and is afforded just over three years to complete it. She pries from the internet a copy of his latest journal article and sifts through it with Ellen. Laced in its pages is a sick irony: he writes, in a painfully long-winded fashion, about how women are seldom believed in cases of sexual harassment. She feels it a poorly disguised cosplay, this man who declares himself a feminist while she—and others—chase doggedly at his heels. She has spent hours before her computer screen with Ellen, the two engaging in robust off-the-record Zoom meetings with his superiors, stating their concerns. The same superiors who assist him onto some lousy podium barely a year later and proudly drape a medal over his neck. The academy all appears a toy chateau to Rose now, with plastic citadels and green synthetic lawns. What does it stand for if it stands for him? Her university once impressed her with its substance. Her tutor, too. She was meant to learn meaty theory there, but not this.

15

It is warm the first day Elsie arrives on campus in 2022. She zigzags through each corridor, taking it all in: its tremendous atmosphere, and so many imposing students, with handsome, strange haircuts and a new kind of put-togetherness, different from before. Having just moved to Melbourne from Sydney, Elsie is to make sense of its edifying counterculture, is to bob her head to new sounds. She is scheduled to meet with Dr Oliver Kerr, the head of the course, to discuss whether to enter the honours program as a first- or second-year student. As Elsie was accepted to study a year prior but opted to defer, Oliver will now decide whether or not she is equipped for such headway. She makes her way to his office and knocks. Oliver is a slim man, with a shiny bald head and kind eyes. 'Take a seat,' he offers. Quickly, he decides that she is primed enough to commence as a second-year student. She had, in the interim, spent a year studying a similar course in Queensland. Despite the honours course in Melbourne having a foundation class in first year that is decidedly formative, Oliver—right then and there—trusted that Elsie could catch up. 'This shaped so much for me,' she admits.

I hear, in Elsie's recollection, proof that exceptions are often made by good teachers for good students. Yes, Oliver is to decide Elsie something of an anomaly, is to determine her bright enough. When Blaine asks me, early on, if all of the women I'm speaking to are gifted, or clever, I nod. In a lot of ways, these women have long come to know that, when it comes to schooling, exceptions are to be made in their presence. Yes, they will read widely. Will warble sweet literary tunes for their superiors. Will be challenged, if given the opportunity. They will balloon out of the staleness of a set curriculum, will come to know that they are the kind to outshine it. Throughout Elsie's degree, Oliver will keep an eye on her. He will put her in touch with other promising past students, will talk with her at length about her struggles, and when the going gets tough, will encourage her to stay. There is too much to lose otherwise.

I, like Elsie, had teachers that made exceptions for me. There was one in particular, Mr Russo. He was an unyielding, handsome man: middle-aged, olive-skinned, difficult-to-crack. Mr Russo had a gameness I found exciting, and quickly did he take a keen liking to me. At the end of Year 11, I bumped into him at the school cafeteria, and—with a knowing smile—he told me he had insisted I be in his English class the following year, so I was. He had demonstrable favourites, a select few he'd call by their last names, almost defiantly, as if they were members of his own nominated bevy of smart girls. One afternoon, he held me back after class to remind me of a quiet, secret truth, a law-of-the-land only we knew. 'Griffiths,' he began. 'You're not like the others.' The connotations were felt by me as a child, even then: I was pert, arrogant, often side-tracked. I'd chew gum and keep my phone within arm's reach, its screen poking out from my pencil case. I'd take silly photos on my MacBook, pulling faces. Invariably, my marks never once toppled. It was important, he had decided, I not let the others in the classroom feel small, insignificant by comparison, given 'how much I was able to get away with'. I stood before him, smug and certain and smart, before he excused me. I was special. Not like the others.

Jade asks me, in one of our many conversations about this book, if I recall the first time I witnessed a teacher having personal boundaries. I am reminded of being on school camp in Year 9. Mrs Howard, an attractive, scanty woman, was leading us through the reeds of a bland hike as we—girls on the brink of womanhood—bored her with our leading questions. One of my friends then—Emma, a pert kid with a thick, brown ponytail who rarely kept her mouth shut—asked Mrs Howard if she was able to recall what her first time was like. Emma, like a few of us, had just started familiarising herself with sex and found it an engrossing topic. Tits, dicks and fluids! What a scrambled big beast of a thing. It gripped her in all of the ways it tends to when you're a teenager, because sex does not wait. It cracks from its shell and makes a mess of your thoughts. It decides it's time to reign with the dawn of a period, or the bashful swell edging out of the boxers of some kid who grinds a little on you in the sunken part of his mother's couch on movie night. Mrs Howard does not answer. Instead, she scolds Emma for having asked it. 'That's inappropriate, Emma,' she hisses. She is not to make an exception, is not to muddy her role as an educator. She is not our mother nor our friend. It's not that Mrs Howard denies ever having had a 'first time', and even as children, we aren't idiots. Of course she has. But in her rejection of the question itself, she insists we aren't meant to see her that way, aren't meant to consider her all sparkly and worn, all body.

In Year 9, Cara—alongside the other girls in her class—had forged a small interest in one of her teachers, Mr Allan. She recalls him being handsome and manly with a throaty British accent. He had hair on his fingers and the back of his hands, and he would not temper his emotions. If he was mad, they were quick to find out. One afternoon, he admitted to a classroom full of fifteen-year-old girls that he wasn't sure if his wife was the love of his life, and each of them cooed, pretending to know what he meant by this.

Then, in Cara's later years, she came to appreciate the quirks and cleverness of her literature teacher, Mr Jansen. He was heavy-set and a little unorthodox, but incredibly smart. She found him compelling nonetheless. The man could teach, and there was much she learned from him. It was only once she left school that he began to divulge to her over Facebook. She received, out of the blue, a message here and there. A seemingly sweet-tempered check-in. One evening, he sent her a long-winded confessional. He admitted that the path of his life had become rocky, unsteady, that he had separated from his wife, had lost a demonstrable amount of weight due to the stress of it all. Cara did not know what to do with this. So she decided not to respond and let his message rot in her inbox instead. What was she to say? What hole did he want her to fill for him? What was it about her that has these men dragooned into some unprovoked candour, has them decide to frolic outside of some boundary line, just to have her hold their sadness for a while?

Exceptions in school are made for the strongest and the weakest of the bunch. The weakest are to be nurtured, if—of course—they're privileged enough. Their strains are to be brought up in parent–teacher interviews so everybody knows how important it is for them to be given supplemental aid. Good teachers are careful not to leave the strongest to their own devices, because this is how they stray. The strongest are ruled instead by subtle, knowing winks, will—in the unwritten law—be handed a book or a sprinkling of sheet music from a teacher's private collection, or be told—as I was—that they aren't like the others, so it best they don't carry on as such. Does this mean that implicit in the architecture of any academy, any educational establishment, is a world teeming with unspoken rules and regulations? Shrewd, knowing winks and quiet gestures? A hush-hush canon, as tacit as they come? For something to be unwritten, it is by definition uncharted and unruly. These small gestures tend to fall squarely outside of the margins of teaching, but this does not necessarily render them bad or wicked. Some, if not all, of my fondest memories of school consist of when teachers have made thoughtful exceptions for me. For example, Mrs Gardner, my music teacher, would invite me into her home every Saturday for two sacred months to practise on her grand piano in the lead up to an exam.

I believe we may have attended the opera together once. I am reluctant to declare that a romantic relationship with a tutor, or professor, has the same footprint that these small deeds do. But I am curious as to whether or not there are certain students who take for granted being made an exception. Perhaps there is nothing more exceptional than having been had by a professor. Here, it appears the last door of the antechamber of being rendered remarkable, different. Wise beyond one's years.

Every good teacher knows that an exceptional child ought to be challenged. I don't consider how abrasive it sounds until I write it out like that: an-exceptional-child-ought-to-be-challenged. Out of context, it reeks a little in ways it didn't before. On one of their many nights together, Cara, while playing Ivan in a game of chess, notices how his speech drivels into various languages. Between each rook and bishop, he speaks to her in broken English, and French, and Italian, just because. I consider it strange, almost antisocial behaviour. You cannot argue, let alone chatter, in a language you cannot speak. Here, he challenges her in the nub of some chess game by reminding her that he has all these dialects on his side.

Yes, she has nice lips and keen, soft eyes. But only he has the faraway vernacular to describe her beauty. If he chooses to, of course. He will never sift through the wreck of his wants, will never make them obvious. He will never choose to. But he will remind her, at various junctures, of who—and what—he is, in all of the vowels she cannot register.

If you are the sort of student who a teacher insists ought to be challenged in virtue of your wit or craft, or whatever else there is, you are to surrender to their way of seeing you. You cannot necessarily see what the teacher sees—you are their student, after all—but you are to trust that it is good, significant. Here, the student is to blindly follow the teacher into their magnificent gorge, is to have faith in their acknowledgement that 'Yes, I do need to be stimulated. Yes, you are right. And only you know.' You aren't to be sure exactly what that encouragement ought to look like, what it might manifest as. You must, in turn, defer only to how your teacher sees you. The bliss of being smaller, of being pedagogically pocket-sized, is to not be able to see yourself yet. You are only ever to become what you think your teacher sees you as, gleaming ahead of time, in the not-too-distant future. The promise of you made beautiful in their eyes. Ellen, in her conversations with Rose, will admit to rushing to finish a practice exam one afternoon so that Neil—her philosophy teacher in high school—would catch her seated in the courtyard reading *The Poetics of Reverie*. 'Look,' she motions, with each turned page. 'I am so young and so full of substance. And really, am I even that young?'

Rose will notice how she comes to reject Samuel's deference of her. How, once she ends her relationship with him, she shaves her head, feels the weight of her girlness a crushing, obvious load. She will dress herself in oversized bombers and think only cruel thoughts when she considers how she was in his classroom: her tiny, neat bob; her small wrists; her fond eyes. She is heavier now, all red-blooded and bold. She is not to be in his line of sight any longer, will not remain as teensy and frail and pretty as the others he will eventually come to hold. No, he did not make her this way. But he found her like this, and she will come to enjoy the preciseness of shedding her skin once it is over, of outgrowing him. If she had known that she was leaving her pelt behind, that it would become parasitic in his care, she would have disposed of it better. She had not imagined it the kind of casing one would endeavour to occupy in due time. Her lowly self made a costume.

In 2020, Ellen—running a philosophy support group alongside Samuel—receives an email from an address titled 'Not Telling'. It details Samuel's conduct in class: his teasing, his flirtatiousness.

'It should be of interest to you to know that one of your committee members has gained a reputation of being inappropriate towards students,' it reads. 'Specifically, by talking about inappropriate topics (e.g., drugs, partying, relationships) during tutorials and becoming "too familiar" with students in general. It is known that he has slept with his former students in the past, and attended student parties too.'

She winnows through it meticulously and takes it to Rose, unsure how best to manage it. This is how it begins. Samuel self-flagellates. He bleats his wet tears and arrives in front of Ellen, sorry. Mainly, he admits, he is apologising due to the administrative headache of it all. He promises to change and takes this as proof of some sour prophesy having caught up with him, and—worse—Ellen and Rose believe him then.

They consider him a man remorseful. It seems thorny for Rose today to rehash this period of her life, how willing she was then to believe him. But as Helen Garner writes in *The First Stone*, 'even a dog gets two bites, before they put him down.'

Ellen trusts, having taken the complaint to Sheila, Samuel's PhD supervisor, that a disciplinary undertaking—sufficient, but not undue—will commence. What she finds out, four years later, when she unearths the notice from Not Telling in her complaints procedure, is how Sheila met Samuel with open, warm arms, like that of a mother. She made him her exception. Over coffee, she told him not to fret. 'The tides of social order are in a constant state of flux,' Sheila insisted, stressing that this small grumble won't tarnish him. How right she was. He inaugurates his apology tour, starting with the student he slept with two years after Rose. But he never quite makes his way down the ancient tracks. Rose's nineteen-year-old self waits, but it is as if his admittance is something that time stole. He does not exhume it from its dusty grave, and she does not ask him to. He apologises, yes—for the contents of the email. But there are harder pills to swallow. At twenty-eight years old, Rose cracks her knuckles and assembles together her overdue grievance. This is how I find her: pulsing with the essence of a million organs. Peering out from between the thorns, unfurled.

*

At eleven years old, Blaine meets Peter, her father's colleague of who teaches linguistics at a university level. He is attentive and warm and sees in her, despite her young age, great potential. 'I worshipped him,' she tells me affectionately. Peter was, for Blaine, a paternal figurehead, a giant in his field. In 2017, she bumps into him at a function and gilds him with praise, stresses the great influence he had on her life. He is elated when she does and takes a keen interest in her PhD. Blaine even shows me a photograph of the two together from that evening. I spot in his eyes an obvious warmth. *So that is what pride looks like.* But still, Greg—despite it all—remains emblematic of the discipline for her. She reveres him in similar ways, finds him equally as charismatic and self-assured as Peter. Like Peter, Blaine's father had always found the mechanics of a sentence so interesting, and—if he had lived a different life—she knows he would've loved to have studied English. He insists Blaine gift him her used textbooks come the end of semester to read, and she does.

Blaine too comes to lean on her teachers in high school. Between daily devotions at her Christian college, she finds herself venerating her English teacher, Mrs Malmuth: a short woman with a wiry blonde bob who would adorn her ears with chunky jewellery. Mrs Malmuth is gentle but shrewd and invites Blaine into the enduring world of Georgette Heyer, insisting she let herself be swallowed up by the rich prose and even richer satire. In Blaine's final year of school, she—rundown with a terrible depression—turns to her art teacher. Conscious that she may drop out, he wheedles her from her sadness by way of a ragged hardback book, a graphic novel about a black dog, insisting she flick through it. *You are not alone, don't assume otherwise*, she hears in his gesture. They keep their affections page-bound, Blaine's teachers. And still, their offerings keep her grounded. No, they aren't to bestow on her their own work, their own little comics or diary entries. Greg, instead, insisted she sit on the end of his bed and listen to him play the ukulele one evening, then waited for her to praise him. He recited her his *own* poetry and hoped for applause. This is how she floated around him while the ground beneath her feet fractured. He didn't care to keep her still and set, hadn't thought to consider whether she was able to forge her own path. Instead, he darts out his arm and maybe even notices it become a chink in her road. He thinks it doesn't matter. He insists it is fine, given he is to catch her when she trips.

16

In 2016, over 30,000 students respond to a national independent survey looking at sexual harassment and sexual assault at Australian universities. It is a wide-scale, landmark study that appears on every news channel, and universities around the country appear to tremble in its wake. Its reverberations are felt in the cool air of each college arcade, in every classroom. And yet in 2024, just three weeks prior to writing this, the *Herald Sun* published that this year, Victorian universities alone received over 200 reports from students and staff relating to incidents of sexual harm.

Before embarking on this book and deciding to work with Cara, Elsie, Rose and Blaine, I naively imagined being able to track a professor's eventual demise. I am certain that, just around the corner, a disciplinary example will rear its head for me, will unveil itself. Surely a man—even just one!—has been required to make full a cardboard carton of his career legacy, to drag his feet through the back entrance of some sandstone college, heading sheepishly towards his car. And yet, in my research, I have only stumbled across one realised dismissal, protected by a university eager to stitch together the lips of its student, whom they encouraged to sign an NDA. I am distracted by the longevity of these men, by how impervious they seem. When Elsie recalls Harrison's paranoia about getting caught, I am made weary by the sheer fact that, in all likelihood, he'd have nothing to worry about. I notice a jadedness start to swell in me and even—for a little while—try to tell myself it a useless attitude, that I ought to salvage any kind of hope for a cultural reckoning if I am to stay motivated. But my ambition becomes blunted and my frustration takes over, pulsing of its own accord like a neglected tumour.

One evening, while struggling to sleep, I ask Georgie—who is lying in bed next to me—if I can just air my ill feelings for a moment. 'Of course,' he insists. Nothing eloquent comes out. Instead, I deliver a bullish, rambling stream of anger. For an hour, I will reel on about it, how nullified I am by the haughtiness of these men and the laxity of their universities. Does it not concern at least somebody, anybody, that there are many tutors who abuse their position of power for their own sexual gratification? I feel I am screaming into some desolate field, that I am following a trail of obvious crumbs and watching others—women not dissimilar to me—hand-pick each one behind me, set it aside and hope for the best. Are we all that starry-eyed to think that lack of consent is the only antecedent for bad behaviour, for an injustice to have taken place? And what about the other students, the ones who aren't game or special enough to be held? How are they to feel if watching this take place from some stale periphery?

Not Telling will stress in her email to Ellen that she believes it is the university's responsibility to 'make sure students (women in particular) feel that their tutors pay them attention on the basis of intellectual undertakings, rather than potential romantic or social interest.' In this admission, I hear—straight from the student's mouth—that this issue has less to do with the relationships themselves and more to do with the criterion they set. Their genesis. What is this criterion, exactly? Recently, while I was in an Uber, the driver cast his eyes across my legs. He was not shy. With an impolite smile, he asked to see where the snake tattooed on my upper thigh began, which would involve peeling my skirt from its post and revealing myself to him. In the passenger seat of his car, I am reminded of the cry of womanhood, of how it speaks louder than much else, distracts the world at large. It can feel so visceral, as if fusty steam is to rise from my lap when he catches a peek. Over a decade ago, while in my once-upon-a-time tutor's classroom, I tactically postured my body into its most ingratiating forms, careful only to be looked at on my good, better side. I was so aware then of my appearance and not much else. It's not as if my tutor had insisted I comb mascara through my lashes each morning or pronounce my answers with a kittenish undertone. The work was already being done for him. No, it wasn't his fault. Not yet. But how different things could've been if he had been heedful to his manner with female students. He was so come-hither, and I was so susceptible to it.

Is it unfair to set a genderless standard onto a university classroom? No, I don't think so. Aspirational, maybe. But isn't that entirely what universities ought to be in an ideal world? Isn't it where we are meant to count the deep sores of civilisation so we are able to pull them apart, one by one? And really, if it weren't about gender, wouldn't there be an equally crowing group of male students-turned-lovers, glued to some institutional fallout between staff and the young men they teach? I am not denying that this hasn't happened and won't again. But I refuse to let the sheer quota of female students who have recounted to me stories of being procured and plucked by their professors go unnoticed. I care to anatomise the wants of a man hellbent on noticing only the young women in this class.

However, in March 2023, a profile in *The New Yorker* detailing philosopher Agnes Callard's unwavering love for Arnold Brooks, her graduate student, piques my interest after having done the rounds online. Callard considers herself probing when it comes to the nature of human conventions, particularly the ones she takes each of us to have intuitively copied. 'To celebrate the end of the term, Agnes had made cookies for her students, and she gave an extra one to Arnold, a twenty-seven-year-old with wavy hair that fell to his shoulders, who was in his first year of the graduate program in philosophy,' it reads, and I scoff. Callard eventually recuses herself from having official academic authority over Brooks and pursues a romantic relationship with him. How it is written—their seemingly irregular origin story—feels glib and doting. Somewhere between being fed a tale pronounced as star-crossed and delightfully cute, I close the tab. Perhaps we are still less familiar with female desire so that we relish its presence at all costs. But male desire often makes for humiliating choices. We know it, in that we feel it. We have come to learn it makes for a febrile, hot mess if in the wrong hands.

Once Greg forces Blaine to have sex with him, she feels he has sliced through her fragile lust and crushed it. Admittedly, her want for him was hanging on by a thread, but this act of swinish hunger made thick her disdain. She decides to end it with him. Oh, how he hates it. How unfair for the enchanted student to stand before him now, bored and yawning. He, in turn, invites her to join him on a field trip to Rockhampton, in the north of Queensland, under the guise of academic alliance. Blaine accepts his offer, curious about the nature of his fieldwork, and the two scramble into his 4WD to undertake a week-long expedition. Given Greg's standing at the university, his trip is entirely recompensed. Every fuel docket, every small slice of pie is logged and reimbursed. Despite this, Greg is careful in how readily he puts his hand in his pocket for Blaine. She treats him nonetheless. She pays for the two to stay a night in a riverside hotel with a big crystal-blue pool and uses her tottery student money to treat him to a lavish dinner. One morning, she adjusts her shorts and wipes a stamp of sweat from her forehead before jumping out of the passenger seat of his 4WD to pick up two pastries and coffees from a small outback cafe. 'Is this your bid to make up for lunch yesterday?' he retorts with a derisive smile, before splitting a sachet of tomato sauce onto his sausage roll and taking a tremendous bite. 'Everything he could get back from the university. I was a student. I felt so stung,' she tells me.

At the tail end of their trip, the engine of his 4WD spits and gags, and they find themselves stuck in the viscid air of outback Queensland, unsure what to do. The sun collapses into the brink of dusk, and they decide to fold down his car seats and make a lousy bed out of the boot. As she welcomes the soft rhythms of sleep, she starts to feel the older married man edging closer to her, jostling up against the underside of her body with hot eagerness. He rattles and rattles and places his hand between her closed thighs, and she snaps. 'Will you just fucking cut it out?' she hisses, turning to face him. He appears so small, so dejected when she says this, and for a moment—just before his eyes start to well—she feels sorry for him. But quickly she imagines his arrogant strut, how sure of himself he is when bolstered at the head of some venomous lectern. Is it so difficult for this man to deny himself of his wants for just a short while? Can he not let the beast of his desire sleep in its wretched hut, or is it always here with him? Greg wails softly into the night before falling asleep, and Blaine disregards his whimpers, finding it all so pitiful.

The next day, Greg manages to kickstart his engine and the two set off again, stopping only for snacks and petrol at a modest service station. Blaine coos at a local grocer cat and gently scratches the underside of its ears while Greg pays for fuel. On their way back to town, the two stop over at Blaine's parents' house. Her mother answers the door, excusing the mess: the abandoned awnings and cruddy makeshift renovations, the endless junk.

It feels odd—a little unsettling, if anything—for Greg to see the shadows of Blaine's past, the disarray of her family home. But, disgruntled, she doesn't care to ask what he makes of it all, is hardly interested in how he sees her anymore. Greg is cordial and magnetic. He uses his big, burly hands to speak and makes her parents laugh. They are demonstrably impressed with his way of being, and over dinner he theatrically recounts some story as they watch, transfixed. Later, Blaine's mother asks her if something happened between the two of them, something bad, and Blaine says quietly, 'Yes. Yes, but I don't want to talk about it.' Her mother never raises it again.

The next day, after arriving back home and while stationed at a sodden park that brims with the eerie murmur of a hundred mosquitoes, Greg offers Blaine his commitment. 'If you want to be with me, Blaine … I might just leave Charlotte. I just need to know if that is something you want,' he says. Furious, Blaine slaps at a small, penetrating insect that hovers above her ankle and looks squarely at Greg. 'Your marriage has nothing to do with me,' she spits.

This last-ditch attempt doesn't save him. The marshy land upon which he announces it speaks louder than his idle words, reveals more clearly to Blaine the miry swamp upon which they have long played. Her legs will be spotty and itchy for days, and still—for four more months—Greg insists she join him back in his bed, the same one he shares with his wife. It is only when she meets James that Greg retreats into the background. He could shrug off her wants at every juncture, particularly her desire to say no—could decide for her, as teachers do, what she is to aspire towards. Until Blaine is held by some other man, he will treat her like fair game.

There is another student, Fran, I speak to while writing this book. She recounts a similar trajectory, a professor who falls into the cataracts of his desires with her only to make a mess of them. Like Greg, he allows his rebel wants to unfurl into an assault. Is it that surprising that a man who gambols about in the swamp of some questionable moral code may end up bogging his student down, will make her muddied with the excess of something stickier, more terrible? Fran, a student at

Elsie's university, meets William as an undergraduate, when she is twenty-one years old. While enrolled in an Economics course, she is required to embark on a mini-thesis, which he is to supervise given he is the senior lecturer. At thirty-nine years old, he boasts quite a luscious head of hair, something she recalls a lot of the other students playfully making fun of him for. Together, they unpack the muscle of her dissertation in many one-on-one meetings. At some stage during the semester, she—and the rest of her cohort, as well as some of their tutors—mosey down to Workshop Bar where, between drinks, he testifies to his impulses and tries to kiss her right then and there, squarely in the eyeline of many other students. It is all so obvious and unchecked. Until it isn't, when a hefty security guard ushers his limp, rollicking body down the stairs of the venue, insisting he is too drunk to be there. Fran, electric with curiosity, finds his Facebook page later that evening while lined up at a kebab shop, her weight swaying between each leg. She messages him, but it ends up hauled into some mysterious, unattended folder. Two days later, in the sobering Sunday afternoon light, she reaches out via her student email instead. 'I'm keen if you are. Want to get a drink sometime?'

It happens quickly. He accompanies her home after drinks one night to her crowded, makeshift sharehouse in Thornbury. The elephant in the room of his presence is heightened, given one of her housemates is also one of his students, and neither party knows what to do with the dragging weight of this information, with how patent and conspicuous their dalliance is. Each time she enters his office during the week, Fran closes the door behind her. William gnaws listlessly at her neck. He even lets his hands venture elsewhere. This is how he relishes making greasy and watering the soil of his private locus, some carved-out erotic wonderland, in among his teeming workplace. Soon enough, her degree becomes signposted by this flimsy lust, and during a final cohort awards ceremony, after having texted each other throughout the entire evening, they sneak out afterwards to fuck. 'It was all very sexy and clandestine, while still in the parameters of a university environment,' she tells me.

Six or seven months of their unruly routine pass. Then, for a few years, they dip in and out of each other's lives. Over the phone, and only if drunk, William shares his day-to-day dilemmas. He admits to being sad and lonely. She comes to learn of a separation. Of the stresses of having two young children. It seems he is always pulling some trench coat and a handful of kitchen supplies out of a duffel bag as he traverses between suburban units.

She refers to their last meeting, some four or five years ago, as 'the grim final act'. I make a note of this, underlining it twice. He meets her at the Marquis of Lorne and insists they each get as boozy as they can. Like clockwork, two drinks continue emerging at their table, and Fran, already drunk, wants to slow down. It is there, in some dimly lit corner, that he forces himself on top of her. She remembers still the rough bite of his touch, how wolfish he became. Insistent, she leaves that evening. She waits for him to go to the bathroom, and when he does, she bolts from the venue. But the memory of her assault remains for years to come. It twists the cold arm of each of their meetings, as if a thing that peers out and taunts her from the lip of his office briefcase, way back when. Or from behind some lone trinket that sat atop a rusted sharehouse bookshelf. It says, 'Listen carefully: it was always going to end like this.'

Two years later, she submits a complaint to her university. 'If he hadn't assaulted me, I probably would've just left it,' she admits. But she feels then she is the possessor of some obligation, some duty. She undertakes an honest mission and returns to her cohort with a span of questions, endeavouring to make a map of his indiscretions, expectant to find she isn't the only one. Hearsay patronises Fran, and she catches—in most corners of the department—a small whisper, something nameless and faceless that utters, 'Well, yes. William is a flirt.' As she assembles her evidence, she realises that the night he assaulted her was the first instance she had ever said no to him, and some script she had memorised will beg she revise it, as if—at so many odd and furtive intersections—she, at twenty-one, had convinced herself that she held all the power. Hindsight, in many of these cases, appears a fierce glare, a blaze in the night that no lowered curtain can disguise, despite its best efforts.

Women will be made to desperately reckon with their younger selves. To squeeze their soft upper arms and shake them, before heaving them into some tight, wily embrace and holding them still.

The day after the assault, William messages Fran feverishly, charged with worry. But he is careful and—in his string of messages—does not admit guilt, despite pleading for some level of forgiveness. Their text thread is marked with understated caution, given how conscious both parties were to not be found out. It does not writhe alive with much proof of their relationship, and only when Fran is required to collate her evidence does she realise the burden of this. Her university tells her that they will communicate with him about her complaint, and then they recede from her view. They do not think—nor care—to update her. Never does she hear from them again. Here, they hold on to photocopies of her diary entries detailing the sex her and him had in his office, messages between the two that discussed his penis, and other deeply personal ledgers from her life. Still, they leave her hanging. 'There's no closure. I would often fantasise about his reckoning', she admits. While writing this, I search his name online and feel—upon seeing his glassy smile—the sharp cramp of injustice. He is still employed by the same university, still as revered as before. Just last week, he spoke to a crowded room of students at a conference in South Korea. Fran is to empty herself inside out, is to be touched in all of the ways that hurt. He, instead, is to remain untouchable.

17

I AM SEATED AT Beare Park, where a small portal to a petite expanse of beach makes itself available to Fil, my dog, who digs madly in the sand. Each of us catches our breath. We take a seat on the nearby grass and it is then that Fil and I in turn are approached by an older man wearing a neckerchief and a trim blue dress shirt. He is postured as wealthy and important and seems to be taking a gentle stroll in the sunlight with his granddaughter, a girl who looks no older than nineteen. 'A wolf!' he exclaims upon seeing Fil, and, agitated, Fil begins to bark, making the old man flinch. Nervous and a little embarrassed, the old man says, 'My name is Wolf, perhaps he's threatened. Two wolves at the park!'

It is only once he meanders away that I realise the woman he is with is not his granddaughter. I watch him place his hand squarely into her back pocket, cup her arse and ask her if she likes boats. Wolf's unease at being frightened of Fil appears to me a little cheap and creaky now. He is the older man—with a name like *Wolf*, for fuck's sake—wanting to demonstrate power and mastery, and yet he trembles at the sound of a measly howl. I hated seeing his ego shrivel up and die in front of me, and I am not the one he is to pour an expensive glass of wine for that evening. I start a new note in my phone and write: 'Is admiration intoxicating? How important is it that these professors retain that, in the eyes of their students? For both parties?'

Around the time Cara finishes university, she is put forward for an exciting job by an associate to work under a man named John Bates. 'He is looking for a young person to come and build him a database from scratch. An artist database. I've arranged for you to have an interview with him next Monday,' her associate tells her matter of fact. Cara quickly searches him online and discovers a man shrouded in legitimacy and ineffable wealth. He is a billionaire, cradled by extravagance. She arrives at his office the following Monday, dressed in her most expensive slacks, red in the face. She is required to pass through two security checks before she can sit opposite him in his top-floor headquarters—encircled by a sublime 360-degree view of the city—as he reels off the names of artists she is unfamiliar with and sternly makes his demands known. She can't quite stomach the news when his assistant calls her the following week and offers her the position. The first thing she does is head into the National Gallery of Victoria bookstore and purchase an A–Z coffee-table record of influential Australian contemporary artists. She carries it to and from work like a bible.

For four long years, John trusts Cara with the back end of his hobby project, and she considers him a God-like figure, the first person to ever say to her, 'I'm giving you an opportunity, here. And I'm trusting you to do it right.' He is exceptional, and devastatingly important. Around John, Cara feels—in her gut—the ripples of his worth. She notices how zealous people are, in his orbit, to shake her hand. 'I loved him,' she admits, with no tang of irony. It is an earnest, gaping love, where he—a man of great acclaim—will endure in her memory as just that: a deity worth admiring.

Eventually, she is offered a job interstate and accepts it. The morning she tells John of her decision to leave, she is jittery, as if nervous to tug on some deep loose thread of home, not ready to see it plummet. In their Zoom meeting, he becomes visibly flustered. He cannot hide his devastation, and she closes her laptop afterwards, places her flushed face into her hands and cries. A few days later, he calls her to apologise and offers his congratulations. It means the world to her to have him say so.

When Cara tells me of John's influence on her life, she speaks with deep reverence. Perhaps because of how caved in to this book I have become, I wait for some penny-drop moment, for her to detail some rueful evening when he—tizzy on champagne—thinks to squeeze the soft of her leg and playfully ask her to sit on his lap. It never comes. He is preserved and all the better for it. Because of this, on her last day as his mentee, she feels genuinely heartbroken, as if having initiated a break-up. 'I was enamoured by him, and still am. I think about him often, if I'm honest. I want his approval, his attention,' she says to me, lovingly. It is a pleasure to write about, if I'm being honest. A purifying sort of love, the sort I care to depict right.

Let's say, though, my suspicions were confirmed: let's say that John had been the sort of man to let some vibrating, fiendish want of his rise above his professionalism, and had—while having encircled Cara in his rich, magnificent world—insisted she join him elsewhere, that they make molten their love. Let's say, for the sake of argument, he had reduced her to sex, had wanted it to outstrip her genuine virtue, the exuberance she brought to that job. I think the damage would've been monstrous. Is there a word to describe the phenomenon of having one's admiration for someone become wrinkled and vile? How important is it that figures of authority are kept bronzed in some glass box, preserved at an arm's length?

One Sunday evening during their relationship, Elsie arrives at Harrison's apartment. She knocks on the door and he doesn't answer but it is unlocked. Elsie proceeds to let herself in and discovers, upon stumbling upstairs, a mezzanine made bottomless with empty beer cans and glass bottles. Harrison is plastered onto his couch. He wakes to find her and continues to drink. 'Every night after that, he'd have one to two bottles of wine, just to himself. There wasn't a night with him where he was sober,' she reflects.

To this day, Harrison's CV boasts many admirable achievements. He, in the course of his career, wins prestigious awards and is bestowed grants that cost the earth. How is Elsie to square the sagging, woozy mess of man she discovers that evening with the one who commands the respect of his roused students in the classroom less than twenty-four hours later? More so, how is she to place herself between his multiplicity of selves? On which ledge is she to tuck away and store her deference to him? It all seems a terrible labyrinth, like a lesson no child cares to learn the first time they perceive their parents as mere people, occasionally shoddy and unfair. How eagerly one may cling to a now-retired aura, knowing full well that they cannot unsee what has already been seen. It is a two-pronged heartache, and Elsie will find herself grieving both the allure of her middle-aged boyfriend, who appears to her now something of a lousy drunk, and the esteem of her tutor, who requires a gallon of booze of an evening just to be.

In 2001, I am seven years old, and my parents introduce me to a new work associate of theirs, an older man with a big burly stomach, a deep voice and a striking presence. Roger is to join their business, and his engagement is one they are hopeful will salve the financial pressures of being young, and acquiring and selling horses bred to race. He is a chef and something of an entrepreneur. He comes to my parents with the proposition of a syndicate, and my father—in his early thirties—is eager to listen, to take his initiative in stride. My parents host monthly events at their stables, where Roger, on the grill, serves up bacon and egg sandwiches, and cajoles prospective owners into buying shares. I view his gusto with pride, and start reaching up and tapping older groups of people on the shoulder, insisting they invest in a racehorse. That I, at seven years old, have read the form guide and can attest to this one or that one's pace and strength—it is all quite cute, but I feel important. Roger winks at me after it appears I have secured some promising deal, and I delight in my specialness. I find him intimidating, but exciting nonetheless.

I notice, as children do, the revere my parents hold towards him, how keen they are to satisfy his vision. One morning, I climb out of bed to hear my mother crying softly while on the phone to Roger, whose resonant shouts I can hear from a distance through the speaker. I am too young to know what the matter is, but am overwhelmed with a deep obvious dislike for the man. This bully! This monstrous bully! I glare at him the next time I see him. I want nothing more than to nail his sorry image to the cross. Perhaps this betrayal is so felt, so memorable to me now, because of the once enormous regard he held in my life. If it had been anybody else, someone less mighty, I may not have even been able to recall the sting I witnessed that day when I clocked his nasty verbal assault on my mother.

Blaine recalls a sharp memory she has of lying in bed with Greg one evening after he had used the bathroom. She notices a small piece of toilet paper stuck to his backside when he returns and finds herself repulsed. When she tells me this, the two of us cackle. What do we make of a man who, once celestial in a lecture hall, has failed to wipe himself properly? He smiles coyly at her, with a piece of damp tissue fastened to his arse like an idiot. He has been returned to a common place. Is just like us. For days I can't unsee it, the image of this mighty, dominant figure turned human in all the ways that sting, by bringing back to his bed the wetted relic of having just taken a shit.

*

While in a relationship with my once-upon-a-time tutor, he requests my help in pitching an article to a public news site. I notice, over the span of a year, his intrigue in how frequently my pitches find themselves accepted, in how outwardly easy it seems to him that I can transmit my views to a wide audience and have them stick. To write for a layperson reader is not usually admired by those in the academic echelon. I recall, at a party with some friends of his, one of them commenting with snark that I write for *VICE*. But I can sniff on my once-upon-a-time tutor his desire to make more known his craft, as many public philosophers have gone on to do. Eagerly, I agree to help. It feels nice to have him see me as a specialist in something.

I begin to edit his pitch only to find it difficult to follow. It is peppered with near-constant philosophical jargon, the kind that can only be understood by a select few. Gently, I suggest he untangle his words a little, and he becomes irate with me. He accuses me of being condescending, and I—shocked—retreat. He says, 'You're treating me like I'm a child who has used finger paint well for the first time. You don't have to be like that.' I notice, in that trivial moment, how easy it is for a man's ego to bruise if challenged. How congealed our dynamic seems to me then, how firmly it has affixed itself to the classroom within which we met. Him only ever as expert.

There are many admirable qualities to an institution that can, and does, rub off on its staff. It is a place, after all, and one can admire a scenery, for example, for its sweeping mass of circuitous bush. A herd of hoofed beasts as they journey across some beaten field. One can admire these things and not yearn to become them: can observe them keenly and find themselves enamoured with their peerless manner instead, their grace. But a university is different. It thrums with a perplexing frenetic aura. It expects of its attendees, an air of allegiance. It says, *you—like me—are marvellous, and big, and just as immaculate.*

Rose will tell me that Samuel has never had a job elsewhere, has—for the entirety of his working life—surrendered only to this strange, insular chasm. What I hear is that he has never been smeared by the underhanded comments of a bitchy retail worker who comments on how poorly he has folded a hoard of cheap linen shirts in a dusty suburban mall. Has never found his fingers wrinkly after preparing a hundred sweet smoothies in the sterile lighting of a juice bar. He has never been second rate. Even as a Master's student, he is to command the attention of a younger, more impressionable cohort of undergraduates, to be admired always. What does this do to a person?

For a moment, I consider it unusual that four men, each prolific in their chosen academic pursuits, would risk placing wagers on their honour, even for the sake of love. But isn't that a familiar old chestnut? The men at the top of their ranks, who pray at the altar of their wants, only to call in sick come confession? It is as if, when power and the most noxious of masculinities become interwoven, risk is an accepted path. The same stale plot lives in every nexus of prestige where men reign supreme: Hollywood, Wall Street, Silicon Valley, the newsroom. It is a familiar recital that boasts—like clockwork—a tired script, a screenplay littered with stock phrases. Do they not fear the yawning disdain of their crowd? How boring it all is.

In late 2024, Blaine arrives at her father's house, equipped with a glum mission. She is to help him renovate his study, which involves clearing his den of empty begrimed jars, ice-cream tubs of food scraps and the occasional enduring gazette from a bygone era, now tea-stained and soggy. She dusts the keys of his piano and peels a discoloured tablecloth from his kitchen table. Beneath it she finds an old birthday card from Greg, addressed to her way back in 2016. It causes her to wince with embarrassment. I count an undue number of xs and os in the photo of the card she sends me and notice his accentuations, how he will underline an occasional word for emphasis. On the top of the card is a quote from one of Shakespeare's contemporaries, Christopher Marlowe. At the bottom, a quote from Ursula K. Le Guin. Beneath it he writes in brackets, 'Yes. I'm quoting a book you lent me' with a smiley face: underlining both the *you*, and the *me*, as if to stress its rarity. A kind, albeit surprising thing.

Here the man admits that, despite being the expert, he is to bow to Blaine's suggestion. I find it so condescending. I am reminded of my once-upon-a-time tutor, and how soured he was when I expected him to adhere to my guidance. Somewhere along the way, students-turned-lovers can forget what they are for. When I ask Blaine about Greg's need for admiration, she puts forward, 'I feel certain that it's this want to be different and especially special that actually underlies the need to be admired and desired, in some way. The tortured philosopher, with an openness to out-of-the-box relationships. Yet at some stage you realise you're very much in the box they placed you in.'

Blaine proceeds long into her day, scrubbing the counters of their shameful avowals, and does so with a big striking smile so as not to mortify her father. She collapses onto his couch and places her tired feet on his coffee table, taking a breath. Then she laughs.

How did we get here? she thinks to herself as she scrutinises her surroundings. To find the heirloom of her and Greg's sordid love beneath the thin skin of her father's disarray is to see it for what it is, for what it remains. It sits among the dregs of other things. It staggers out from the offscourings of life itself. How many other small parts of her can she find in this mess? How many report cards and dusty photographs and CDs from her elementary years, signposted and lodged in the pit of her family's archive? Only once it shrivels up does it become hers. The corner of the card is stained, so that some of Greg's ballpoint confessions have become babbled and botched. Perhaps her father had let a drop of water from a nearby glass spill out onto it. And—without anybody's knowledge—had made clouded and blurry Greg's quoting of marvellous other thinkers. Or perhaps the card had been delivered to Blaine as such. She isn't to know. All she does know is that somewhere along the tracks of Greg's professorship, his wants had splattered from their vessel and made a mess of his words. This is how they'll remain to her now. The blurry corpse of some strange distant thing, jammed among the dense corpses of other things in a home she cares not to enter if she can avoid it. A home full to the brim with someone else's mess.

18

I HAVE SPENT MUCH of the last year lurking. Through hearsay, I will sniff out a name, and scrabble about in the crowded aisle of a bookstore, for example. Will attend the launch of a poetry book, where a professor I know to have fucked his student is hosting. I will watch his every last motion: how he gears himself up between questions, how enrapt he appears in his female subject, how he crosses his long, scraggy legs. What is it that I expect to find? I raise my heels a little and amble through the venue, as if he is a bomb awaiting detonation, and I the seasoned security officer, entrusted with an honest task. I will return—again, and again—to the pub he frequents, until others notice and raise their eyebrows. I will catch wind of a photographer, who has boasted before to a woman I know about sleeping with students he has previously shot, and I will reach out to request headshots. He will accept, and come the sixth relatively flirtatious voice-memo I receive, I will call it off, nervous. I notice, eight months in, something akin to homesickness, a rushed pang of wanting to return somewhere that isn't here, to the repose of having once been less suspicious, less scheming.

Perhaps I have always schemed when it comes to this. Yes, I have schemed before, from a less honourable, more naive stoop. Around a decade ago, I would carefully plot my tutor's whereabouts, choreograph my on-campus movements so as to spring up in his line of sight, to make myself seeable to him. He would be seated on campus, eating his lunch, and I'd be two rows in front. Every week, I'd map out my university's acreage, would write in my diary, 'If my tutor were just to ask me out for a drink! If only! God, if only.' Today, I am still conspiring in the same realm of power and desire he and I have long played in, only from the other side. Back then, I hoped that if he'd just see me, he'd notice how easy it could be to love me, would imagine—with me—some big, beautiful life. That he did. Now, he does not return my messages. Now, all I have is this tired investigation, is the prickly embrace of suspicion. Age and rage and time have made me blunted. I am older now, and biting. Too old, I think, to ever stumble into the well of this phenomenon again. Too old to not want to claw my way out, to reach into the damp shaft and offer younger, more hopeful women a grave hand. Jade asks me one evening if back then, when my once-upon-a-time tutor and I started dating, I'd ever have registered it as wrong. 'No chance in hell,' I tell her. I remember in 2016, a few months after we commenced our relationship, reading an article published in the now defunct *The Lifted Brow* that detailed a repulsive display of power and abuse from the anonymously penned perspective of a student who had been pursued by her professor. *Thank goodness that's not us*, I thought to myself then.

I have heard of relationships that have begun here and not crumbled. Relationships made up of the same bones and muscle. A few, here and there, have declared themselves avowedly good, have boasted being cleansed of inequity. Why, then, am I so reluctant to believe it possible? Is it because I too have felt like the exception to the rule until I found—tucked beneath some wayward comment or the sum and substance of time—that I was the rule all along? For me, it came with my ex-partner's recruitment of another student during the tail end of our separation, then another again years later. There was nothing he could have said to relieve me of my concerns. Though I decided to love him, I did not also decide to sign up to some small but mighty harem. He had offered, through his enlisting of others, proof of something dubious and suspect. All I had to do was notice.

How humiliating it is, to notice. To notice what has always been there, skulking about in the fine print. It is not to be smacked in the face with new, ravaging information. It is to realise that one has had her eyes shut, has even made garish and presentable an ugly truth, which is worse. When Elsie first notices, she is still a student, still Harrison's student. She is piecing together the finishing touches of her final work in an enduring daze, as is the nature of any deadline. Hours melt leadenly into each other as she binds herself doggedly to her legacy. When she eventually presents her work to her judging panel, Harrison is there—on the panel, of course!—and he is nervous. Amelia, too, who extols Elsie for her mastery, who even says, 'Now it's your turn to join us. Welcome to the industry, Elsie.' To not be on campus half as much is to see Harrison less and less. Elsie notices that her studentship has come to encase their strange love, and that same love becomes limp if made to stand on its own. She begins to see him only once every two weeks instead. It is all so intermittent, so disorganised. 'It was scary for me. As soon as he wasn't my tutor anymore, he wasn't there,' she tells me. Overwhelmed by having noticed this, she arrives at his apartment one evening and decides to call it off. He is a little sloshed when she does and hugs her with equal parts muffled want and resignation. She has graduated, and the coil of their bond has as well. This he accepts. The end is messy, and she materialises in his bed once more a few months later. It doesn't ever feel the same, though. They sleep together, and he offers—come midnight—to call her a cab, and she grimaces at the thought of being made so transient, so temporary. The following year, she spots him at a gallery opening, and he offers her a mousy smile. She does not smile back. It is then that she sees how his face contorts, how it wrenches into terror among the crowd. He looks upon her as if she is a ghost, a terrible wraith who flicks at the light switch and coos in the night until he can no longer take it.

What is the great loss if we are to, say, outright prohibit these relationships in Australian universities? In the UK, University College London is the third university to ban sexual and romantic relationships between staff and students. While many institutions appear to be protective of personal freedoms, in 2018, the 1752 Group and the National Union of Students published a survey of 1839 students, documenting that four-fifths of them were uncomfortable with staff having relationships with students, describing them as 'predatory'. I am not foolish and am sure that an outright ban would not keep speckless the university breeding ground. But would it not encourage, at least, some small cultural shift? Would it not allow students the reprieve they are rarely afforded when it comes to making sense of the muck of these entanglements? And is it love we are protecting—or something else entirely—if we are reluctant to outlaw these romances, to turn a blind eye to their genesis?

All of us, when it comes to love, are to bob along the long ocean trench of it, unsure as to where its deepness lives. Perhaps what I am saying is that love is temperamental at the best of times. This is its only certainty. But when it comes to relationships between professors and their students, we have the cold, frank data to prove at least one fact: that students of all kinds are to be impacted by their presence. Even the students that do not drown but who observe from the dry shoreline the big wet of it all. 'If he loves her, why not me?' they will ask, rubbing sand across the crisp of their thighs. And then there's the ones whose feet never quite touch the ground, who will grub about in the yawning reservoir for a lone branch. Who may even find one in the faithful shape of some previous one. Some familiar, wooden limb. 'If he could love me, if he could see me, why not the other teachers?'

*

Come October, Rose anticipates the birth of Samuel's baby. She sleuths Facebook for any small proof she can muster and finds—on Samuel's mother's page—a photograph of teether toys, a tiny onesie, and more. 'Not long now,' the caption reads excitedly. For a long time, she imagines the hideous load of her memory as a thing he is to tow around. This is her gift to him. 'I'm such a pest,' she laughs, detailing to me how many forceful emails she has sent, how many department heads at Samuel's university have come to know her name. She becomes used to being ignored, so much so that it doesn't ache anymore. It just is. Ellen is her silver lining. Their friendship has become the buttress of this inglorious process, has made her feel less alone. 'Do you think I should send him a copy of this book once it's finished?' she asks me one evening. 'I don't have his address, but I could send it to his university pigeonhole or something,' she reflects dreamily.

I don't know what to say to this. There is something quite glum about imagining Rose cradling this investigation in the omission of everything and anything else. He is to tend to the wails of his youngster, and Rose is instead to cling to some paper trail of badness, the bound and formalised ledger of some interlude of her twenties, her life, as if it is anything at all to him. At every juncture, she and Ellen muster up some evidence and giggle to themselves, as if to say, 'This'll do it.' It never does. He continues on, braced by the warm steadfastness of his institution, and they will—and do—go to bed hungry.

*

As I write this, a professor is standing before a gaggle of young hopefuls, pointing to a parroted quote from a book his students will have thought they understood until now. This is because he decodes it new. He wheels his way inside the text and links arms with the author, as if he a man at a party full of somebodies, and so are you, and here this man insists you ought to meet so-and-so, that you two would surely get along. You will forget this, as his student. Will forget you are his student. And you will think that this is the nature of any rollicking, good scholar. A good teacher will surely have you fall in love with him, will be a man able to melt away the boundary lines and see you as all brawn and brains, as the same as him and Shakespeare, or Foucault, or Chaucer, or whoever else he has led to the party. You will forget that he is just a man who wakes every morning needing to piss, who will find on his calf an itch worth scratching, a lone pimple on his neck. Or perhaps you don't forget. You place your rough nails upon your own leg and think of him. You consider the bricks and pillars of this classroom so draconian, so unfair. You could've met elsewhere and cut through the bullshit of this deep, cavernous want together. That's what you tell yourself, yes? Only later, when you wrench out a grey hair from your fringe—or, like me, look upon the outline of your love as it is told back to you by way of four other women's stories—will you realise that this romance was buoyed up only by such arbitrary furniture, by the U-shaped configuration of a discussion group. No, sweetheart. He never would've spotted you across the counter of a tiring bar, despite how handsome your face would've looked under the warm red lights. But bigger again, you never would've cared to look for him. Never would've spotted him either. He'd be as musty, as boring, as the others out there in the real world. Here, in his amusement park of wants, is where he will find you, as he has done before, and as he will do again.

Somebody will ask me, while writing this book, if I am only looking at heterosexual dynamics. Well, yes. But the straightness of the relationships I have decided to focus on is not necessarily meant to be pontifical. It is just so easy, I think, for relationships such as this to swamp about in the underlay of heterosexual mishaps, for their manuscripts to be so trite and glaring. Are they not just machines for which gender is reproduced tirelessly? For which a man can have his man-ness a thing that swaggers as it sways, and a woman can have her woman-ness condensed and restless, so painfully and so obviously up for grabs? If you peruse the wreck of some of the most boring gender prescriptions, you will find in its debris something not too dissimilar to this. If gender doesn't matter, if it wasn't the cartoon kingdom upon which these relationships burst forth from their soil, why are there significantly more instances of male tutors who procure sex and love with female students?

And where, I'd like to ask these institutions, are these students to go? Where do they go? Elsie has found that the warm welcome to the arts world she was promised has not come to fruition. Rose is to wither into the nullity of her degree, one she barely obtains. Blaine is to be burdened by some dreadful knowledge, like a ravenous spy who leers upon Greg as he roves through her student body in more ways than one. As for Cara? Cara is to turn inwards instead, to ruminate over Ivan for years to come, never knowing who or what she is to him.

I will wake in the middle of the night, vexed, feeling like a hyphen between two words. Sometimes it is not all bad. But rarely is it ever all good. Tired of it all, I decide to file a complaint against my once-upon-a-time tutor. I do the administrative rounds and make my name known to his superiors. I file my paperwork and offer up my findings. His position as professor is made permanent not long after my complaint is recorded, and I am ushered back into the idleness of whatever else there is, whatever else remains.

An acquaintance tells me that, as a sessional tutor, she is to complete an integrity module at her university. I'm curious as to how it differs from the integrity modules at Blaine's university. It flirts with the topic of staff–student relationships, even encouraging tutors to not sleep with their students if—of course—they can help it. But if they do, it's best they report it to management as soon as possible. She admits that there was more effort put into a slide on fire exits than this. She stresses this because it is absurd. Because the threat of students being engulfed by something far hotter and more ravenous than a fire remains. For this, universities offer no clean escape route. There are no suitable alarms to sound, no arcane passageways to usher students into sans smoke and flames.

Another acquaintance tells me that, as a psychologist, they are subject to incredibly strict rules surrounding intimacy and love with one's clients. 'Oh, but aren't you all adults?' my galling devil's advocate scoffs from the grotto of my mind. Not because I believe it. I am just frustrated that a professor who falls in love with his student is not considered as much of a pervert as, say, a psychologist who falls in love with his patient. Isn't it all just as corrupt? A quality teacher, like any quality psychologist, is to consider the value of failure, of deficiency in his student or patient. The classroom is a potent place, where outlooks are to be challenged, doused with more sturdily built viewpoints. A classroom, particularly one in which gender and race and sex are chewed over critically, is where a student ought to discover herself.

No, students aren't meant to be perfect. Neither, I am sure, are patients. If anything, they are meant to be pliable and honest. To arrive at their session doors eager to be changed. We bring to these realms the burning questions we have about ourselves, about how the world works and how—if we're lucky—we learn it ought to work instead. What, then, are we teaching students by making these relationships permissible?

For a long while, I believed that my once-upon-a-time tutor saw through some high-handed glass box in how he saw me. That I had a shine so glaring, so scintillating, it could not help but reflect off whatever crate I was held in. But what if that crate was where the beauty lived all along, in that it preserved something sacred, something meant to be unimpeachable? If love is born out of the classroom, it is a thing that chips and nicks at the glass of this box, and I am reluctant to think anything such as this, anything hellbent on destroying the case within which it sees and likes something, not greedy. Not terribly wrong.

19

Ellen, at eighteen years old, flings her long hair forward. She ties it up into a high ponytail moments before the band starts their set. She is at Cherry Bar in the Melbourne CBD with Con, her literature teacher, who has—upon Ellen graduating high school—invited her to join him at a gig. Her gesture, to draw back her locks the way she does, is so effortless. She makes herself unencumbered with the slender tendrils of her obvious youth, and this he notices. She does not know this then, but tonight marks the beginning of a strange, icky entanglement with the low-lying wants of a man over a decade her senior. He had once requested she, at seventeen years old—

along with the rest of her class—hand in a collection of small, personal essays, reflections on their assigned summer reading, a ledger he promised to read carefully. He fingered through the fuck-you revelations of a kid smart beyond her years, let what she made then of death, of love, of whatever else there is to find in the slums of her girlhood, wash over him. And here, just over a year later, Ellen bobs along in the clammy uproar of a punk gig, careful not to be bumped, as that would mean bumping into him. Here, it is all body. Is it ever not?

Ellen makes do with the flirtatious advances of her once-upon-a-time teacher for a long while afterwards. He places the palm of her hand on him as he throbs on two separate occasions. He tells her he loves her. She returns to her old high school one afternoon to pick up her younger brother. And, on the walk back to her car, Con shyly appears. He circumvents her and admits something horrid. 'My wife is a little uncomfortable with our friendship,' he says.

'That's what does it,' she tells me. It is one thing to be conjured up in the older man's dreams, but to be a foreboding lesson in the older woman's nightmares is to be made real again in all of the ways that beat and whack. She is eighteen years old and a hiccup in a stale marriage. What a foul thing to be.

Technically speaking, Con is no longer Ellen's teacher. He is free now to spill into her, all sweaty and changed, if he sees fit. As is she. But is their freedom ever the same as one another's? I am reluctant to think so. While writing this book, I find myself progressively less charitable when it comes to caring about the autocratic markers of stale employment contracts, of when—or if—it may be bad or wrong to touch according to whether one is still waged to teach. When is injustice—or love, for that matter—ever able to be made sense of entirely according to its technical conditions?

*

I return to the rules to ground myself in something concrete. To find where the technical badness lives. Online, I post a poll: *Should professor/tutor relationships with students in universities be banned outright?* An overwhelming number of *yes*es, a fair few *it depends*, and a small handful of *no*s emerge in response. Somebody puts forward, 'I think it depends where you meet. Were they your professor or tutor first? Or did you meet in another situation that didn't have a power imbalance, and then you attended university?' Another replies with a sequence of voice memos as she walks through a food court. She tells me that her concern with pedagogical relationships is 'the way it predominantly shames and disadvantages young women.' This, I think, is impossible to police. She continues to describe a tutor she had while at university herself, who routinely embarked on relationships with 'slim, hyper-feminine female students'. His department, instead of slapping him on the wrist, eventually only came to him bearing 'lesbian PhD students to supervise, who wouldn't take shit,' she tells me. Somehow, in returning to the black-and-white question of mandated prohibition, of putting a dictum forward to my community, the responses I receive inevitably bleed out and over the boundary lines of my original query. She continues, 'I think it's always the men who weren't hot in high school, who are now powerful and proud and have something to prove, that embark on this behaviour.' Bingo. Here, I stumble upon another question, am made to grapple with a new string of rules. In the sexual economy, who is fuckable? And who is hungry for a small taste of comeuppance?

I have never met a woman who has felt entitled to sex or desire. I have met many who have had to wear the itch and wants of others like a putrid laurel, a plastic tiara not of their own making, as if it were placed upon their pretty little heads long ago. Perhaps in high school.

A professor I know tells me that, while meeting a particularly beautiful Hinge date at a pub in Sydney's Newtown, he noticed the probing eyes of a nearby patron who—when his date journeyed to the bathroom to reapply her lip gloss—asked him, 'What do you do?' Politely, the professor responded with, 'I am a professor at the University of Sydney,' to which his observer smiled coyly and said, 'Well, that makes sense.' He was elated when he told me this, as if it were worth boasting about. Here, the rules of sex are made sagacious and neat. It is an ordinary, unexceptional design: an attractive young woman who shares a bottle of red with a man made robust, larger than himself, by his line of work.

One evening, while chatting with Blaine, she will make mention of something wretched. It stays with me for some time: 'I never really told many people about Greg, because I didn't think people would believe me. I didn't think they would consider me pretty enough.'

In 2015, Greg sends Blaine a message: 'My hot, smart linguistics student cut her hair today.' Taken aback, she responds, 'Now I know you eye off hot, intelligent students.' Half an hour later, he writes, 'You bet I do. And I always have. You, for example.' A punch in the stomach, a rattle in the thorax. She asks him the following day why he thought to bring that up. He apologises and admits it was just an example of the flirtatious, elastic rapport between the two of them, because Blaine—Greg says—has always told him about the men that chase her.

'I don't get that sort of attention,' he blurts out piteously. The men in question, Blaine tells me, consist of a creep she met once at an empty bus stop on a cloudy day who affixed his terrible, keen eyes on her body. She hated it, how unswerving he was, how noticeably desiring. Mousy but polite, Blaine agreed to offer him her email address only once he asked, to which he sent—a week or so later—some base confession, admitting to having fantasised about her.

There were others around that time. Other men who seemed unable to swallow her hints. She reported them to Greg, not as a handful of crushing victories, but instead as hellishly unnerving interactions.

'I certainly wasn't gloating,' she stresses. Greg, however, is unable to tell the difference.

Professors like this will anoint the students they pursue with clean, decided power. *You see the way she waltzes into class, how her stockings overdraw a little at the knees? You see the way she has made me a drivelling mess?* But what is the benefit of such a power if it is so fragile, so up-for-grabs? If a woman is to parry the thirst of others out of fear of violence or harassment, it is a power left shivering and unshielded. She is a naked trooper, out on some treacherous assignment. All brawn, no cannon. I have no doubts that a man who considers himself long robbed of sexual attention will take gusto in being looked at and admired as he rests his weight on a timber rostrum, clears his throat. Here is where he becomes sex in all of the ways he hoped he could as a boy. Here he fucks cheerleaders and forgets to message them back. But his becoming of such is not made tangled and broken by the threat of cruelty, of sexism. The man thinks that to arrive before a blackboard and a small handful of impressionable students is sex, is to have greased his elbows with the remnants of hard, dull work. Hasn't he earned this? Isn't it all just some fringe benefit to being good and smart and prolific and man?

Blaine asks me what I consider beautiful, and it takes me days to respond. I trawl my tongue along the rough of each molar and try to remember. Why is it so difficult to answer? And why is it that Blaine's beauty matters so much to me? I notice this preoccupation of mine when I receive a response from a burner account to my Instagram poll, the one about whether or not pedagogical relationships ought to be banned in universities. It comes from an account with no followers, no posts, no photographs. 'I was in a relationship with my professor and it fucked me up, so yes,' it reads. I eagerly message the account back, asking if they'd be comfortable speaking with me.

'Why not?' she responds, and—like that—another man's hobby horse is to open her mouth, is to make the mess of her twenties known. Her name is Adrienne. We exchange phone numbers, and I never do see her, am not ever able to put a face to the name. What listless truth would I find in being able to decide her pretty enough? Am I just Blaine's fears consummated?

Adrienne recites a familiar story to me. She describes her professor's type: young, slender, undefiled students. The two spend years together after that first portentous evening when he invites her to join him for a drink after class. Adrienne, I come to gather, is cool-headed and insistent. She has a certain spunk about her, the kind that comes from the hard-bitten, salt-stained attitudes of land-strewn parents, people who humbly made an honest living for themselves in some frail country town. She hates the smell of eucalyptus, the arid preachings of Australian bushland. In fact, she finds it all quite depressing. Stanley, her professor, is her ticket out of the cataclysm of farmland. Adrienne is the most beautiful girl in the world to him. 'Girl, not woman,' she stresses to me. Stanley teaches her Fine Arts, and—while completing her studies—Adrienne becomes eager to interrogate girlhood in her practice, to pierce through to the marrow of it. *There has to be more than prettiness,* she thinks. She peels off the grisly tendrils of female disguise—each sinewy off-cut—and offers them up to him for critique. He hates her findings, considers it all a bit ugly. 'More colour, Adrienne. And less feminist theory, please. Show me more of yourself,' he insists, and even becomes irate with her. It's as if he considers her childish and entitled in how she does not relish his feedback.

'What the fuck does he know about girlhood?' she insists to me, now a woman in her thirties.

How freeing it is to lay one's twenties to rest. To not bicker with one's body as much. I am cognisant that, as I write this, I have graduated from the windy testing ground of girlhood. I am not ogled at as much, as scavenged through as I once was. I can feel the hot wants of the world-at-large as it peels its greedy eyes off me and looks for others: younger, more shapable women. I see girls everywhere: lining up to be carded at pub entrances, guffawing with one another over coffee, drudging about in library halls, skittishly filling up their tanks at petrol stations in the dead of night. All of the women I have spoken to as research for this book are to stitch together the cloth of their girlhoods, to pull their costumes out of the cupboard where they hang, and show me their rips and tears. This is how they were found by these men, after all. As girls.

Stanley detests how Adrienne makes a mess of her girlhood. How she invites ink into her skin and holds scissors to her hair. Each small gesture is an affront to him. She finds out, in the middle of her relationship with Stanley, that he had—some years ago—dated another student. An artist. Prolific in her own right. He had even collaborated with her! This discovery pales Adrienne's happiness. It makes her feel a little sick, if she's honest with herself. She brings the news of her uncovering to Stanley with a bite as blatant as they come. When she does, he insists she is different, special. From thereon, she feels the ghost of that crisp, sharp want of his. She finds herself fettered to a terrible pattern. They fight and fight some more. It is as if their belligerence for one another emerges out of thin air, and—because of this—Adrienne ends it. It is all too grubby, too broken.

During the tail end of their relationship, she receives a phone call. Her father has suicided, and she must clean up the smear of his final moments. Numb, she arrives at his home. She swims through the sea of empty alcohol containers that make sticky his floorboards and counters. His red heeler is barking among the glum surroundings. She affixes a rusty leash and keeps the dog for years to come. A handful of police officers are there to escort her to the station, where she is hurtled into answering a gamut of questions. Then she returns to the noiseless scene of her father's death, where she retrieves a Jimmy Steiff teddy bear she had gifted him years prior, a couple of dusty photographs, and some documents. She reaches out to Stanley the following evening, as if compelled to do so. Somehow, he manages to pivot around the terror she has faced and insists that he, too, has wrestled with depression as of late. It is all so selfish, so revolting, that Adrienne hangs up.

Beauty here, where Adrienne is made to sit, is briny and stiff, and she—having left her Blundstones at the door of her mother's house as a teenager—will feel the weight of Stanley's coaxing, how he promised her more than this. How he slung her over his knee and cooed, 'Oh, Adrienne. These people don't get you. Come to the city, come to me, and make a name for yourself.' Her talent, her wit finds itself bleached and beautiful in the hot sunshine of sandstone promise. They all said it would when she was little. So clever, she was. So beyond her years. What they didn't say is that her professor would stand before the shine and cast a shadow no light—no big, magnificent sun—could ever pierce through.

*

Sienna uploads a new profile picture, smiling next to Samuel. It is all so vanilla, so plain, from the outside looking in. Quite simply, it is a photograph of a happy couple and their new dog. Sienna's head is cocked, and she smiles a little as a floundering mess of toffee-coloured puppy jerks about in her arms. Rose brings the screenshot to me over WhatsApp conspiratorially. 'Have a look,' she says. What story is it telling, this snapshot of a quiet life, an uncomplicated union? Rose comes undone a little every time she retrieves it from her phone. Here, she thinks, his new cohort is to assemble around him, posturing as a family. Her own dog snores at the foot of her bed, his legs rickety with age.

'Remember this guy?' she snickers, placing the phone and Samuel's big grin before her dog's half-closed eyes. Her dog does not stir.

Rose once felt she had a kind of magnetising force, could catch men in the teensiest of stares and have them tread on her small, delicate heels. As a child, her mother would plait her hair into tight fishtail braids until her temples started to ache. Then the two would walk, Rose holding her mother's hand as the two cavorted about Kmart together. Rose wincing each time a doting older woman would reach for her delightful pink cheeks and make mention of her prettiness. Oh, how people loved to graze. To make oily her skin with their sullied fingers, just to feel. She catches a glimpse of her reflection in the mirror of her phone, only once it goes black, and sees looking back at her a pair of thin, pursed lips and the shell hole of a hacked-off pimple. It's not that she considers Sienna any more beautiful than her. It's just that she never cared to, was not meant to know Sienna like this. Comparison is a rotten beast, has driven her to some repugnant place.

*

I eventually tell Blaine that, when it comes to beauty, I find authenticity quite arresting. Eccentricity, even. A tree that sheds its leaves unlike any other I've ever seen; or a work of art; or the quaint echo of a stranger's toothy smile, veiled beneath the aberrant layers of a wonky, half-done haircut, that'll do it. Rose, too. So when Samuel decided to make crooked his wants and go looking again in all of the places he shouldn't have, he told her—by way of a new recruit, scoured in the same stomping ground—that she was never special. Never beautiful. He is to wring the wet sponge of her beauty, trap it in a wetted canister and have her make do with its husk. She thumbs the side of her temples, places her phone beside her pillow, closes her eyes and nurses a familiar pang.

20

Cara loves to be left alone. Every morning, she rises before her boyfriend and walks. It is at dawn when the ocean asks for her. It insists she roam towards its marshy foreshore, so she does. Once she arrives, she wets her feet and listens as the sea gurgles its white froth, as it glides a little towards her. Back again it goes, shyly. This is how she tracks its pulse. Her life is punctuated by sleepy, solitary moments. A decade ago, she lay atop her quilt cover and lit a cigarette under the fairy lights of her sharehouse bedroom as the slow hum of cars from the nearby highway crept in through her window. 'This is all mine,' she thought stolidly. There is no need to wedge oneself into life, to busy oneself enough that you become hacked and split in two or three, when all it takes is this: a small juncture, the freedom to just be. When I ask Cara about joy, this is what she tells me. That joy is to be uninterrupted, to submit your body to the ocean breeze, and pause.

There are some people who believe that adults deserve to be left undisturbed when it comes to sex: the sort they hope to have and with who. That, once we graduate into adulthood, we should be able to festoon our wants onto whoever is equally as wanting, regardless of gender, sexual orientation, race, age or ability. Well, yes—is this not how homosexuality was eventually decriminalised? Does this not live impassively in the fever of resurfaced abortion debates, that we ought to keep politics out of the bedroom, to keep consensual sex—and all of its built-in hiccups—unimpeachable? Sure. But something's missing. I am reluctant to assume sex any more liberating for women if we are to, perhaps, just tack on more kinds. I am disinclined to believe it emancipating if we were to simply shrug at the thought of female students fucking their male professors. How often, and how eager, are women to unbind themselves from sex. So why not neuter the classroom and make it so the ideas of female students—not their bodies, per se—remain the most salacious part of their participation? What do we lose here if we abandon sex? Am I prudish to insist that women just be left alone?

A professor eager to hold his student may insist she is a free agent. She may have even slept with many people before him. Sex, he could find himself maintaining, is a familiar homestead, isn't even a place delightfully new or daunting for her to arrive at the doorstep of. 'She, like me, has wants I don't care to patronise, and neither should you,' he may huff and puff. It is all the same from where he stands. Her desires are to spread over him, like a hot air he knows how to recognise, given both he—and her—are adults, after all. To begin the conversation here, at a female student's sexual buoyancy, is to begin the conversation in the wrong place. The classroom is not a place two people arrive at untethered. Their boots have long crunched atop the grit of sex and gender as it stands. It is not his job to remind her of this. No, because he ought to be made busy with his real job, with the task at hand: to teach, and only ever that.

While seated in the courtyard at Barkly Square in Brunswick, I notice a pigeon in the rafters above me as he performs his pesky courtship. He beats his feathers and flails about another bird desperately. I wait for her to take heed, to behold the song and dance of it all. It is spring, a season marked by mating. It is easy to spot. First come the feeble, soft bodies of baby lambs as they shamble towards their mothers in open paddocks, the kind that frame barren highways. Then the hot screeching of suburban mynas who slingshot from their nests of an early evening, determined to browbeat an unassuming dog in its collar and lead as it trots towards the park. Animals, each with a love worth safeguarding, each eager to have it be left alone. Before long, another pigeon joins the long beam, and the male pigeon—flustered—begins again. He does not care to differentiate the two. Flapping a little, he sees only his animal want, feels only the brace of his nature.

*

It is November 2024, and I am nearing this book's finish. It is November, and Rose zips up the fly of her suit pants, wriggles her way into a charming blazer and plugs an unfamiliar address into her phone. Maps says that it will take her twenty-six minutes to get to her destination, so she allows forty-six. A public event is happening in a local bookshop, where Samuel is scheduled to speak to a small, dazzled audience. Rose arrives, sits alone at a neighbouring bar, and sculls a single beer. She washes an expired beta-blocker down with one of eight sips, takes a deep breath and walks. She is not to leave him alone, not yet.

Samuel spots her on first glance as she takes a seat and—with a bemused, irked expression—tracks her movements. Rose sinks into a rickety chair a good seven metres from him as others retrieve bound paper and ballpoint pens from their bags or steadily peel open their laptops. She is not here to learn from him, so she does not require a notepad. Instead, she feels around the room with her eyes, eager to make greasy its walls with each gaze. It is as if it is just the two of them, for the first time in a long time, despite people piling in in small, unassuming droves. The event commences, and before long, Samuel stands to speak. He paces leisurely as his voice permeates the space, taking considered, leaden steps with each sentence. People nod favourably as he makes sweet-sounding his thoughts, and Rose—in two instances—catches herself doing much the same before desisting. She is here to ask a simple question. Once question time arrives, she swallows. She signals towards a student with a microphone, and then—at once—she is holding it.

'Thank you,' she stutters. 'I'm curious.' Another stutter. 'When it comes to making complaints about sexual and romantic relationships between professors and their students...'

The room falls eerily still as university staff—some of whom have archived Rose's complaints, the ones that made for lousy email carcasses that rotted in their inboxes—turn to face her. Samuel's eyes are soft and careful when she speaks. 'What do we do when we feel we have been let down by the institutions we thought would care for us? Students in these situations, I mean.'

Samuel takes a deep breath. She swears it reverberates. This neat, fallen exhale, with its many echoes. In facing him, she has scuttled over the tracks of politeness, has made urgent her presence. Tactless and unrelenting, she feels. Perhaps it's this that causes her chin to quake a little: the unpleasantness of making a room sticky with unanswered pain, the awkwardness of it all. Samuel, in seeing this, offers her a tender, almost fatherly smile before insisting to his crowd it best he don't answer. Left then with the rack and ruin of his silence, she stands and jostles her way towards the door.

Rose, once making herself scarce and pushing gently through the crowd, hears her name uttered behind her as she walks.

'Rose, it's me. It's me,' Samuel pleads. She turns to face him and there he stands, like a small offering. She could make a desperate run for it, but she doesn't. Instead, she accepts his invitation to sit with him for a while. He tells her he understands. 'Yes, of course you feel the way you do,' he maintains. He manages still to bring up how she has become an unshakeable hindrance on his reputation, how he has been made to sit in high-ceilinged offices and plead his case. How he is lucky to have a job. How her efforts have only harmed Sienna, who—bruised—bears the brunt of Rose's testimony.

'You did that, not me,' she spits back. 'You did that, Samuel. You did that when you decided to pursue a relationship with another student.' He nods mechanically, as if referencing a move he had once read in a handbook on how best to pacify a disgruntled lover, but his gesture feels void and wooden. Once his audience filters out from the space, he—distracted—looks around, eager to network. Rose notices this and stands to leave. No longer does she feel the pull of a want for closure, of anything at all. At last, it is over.

END

Desire is an ample thing, made contaminated by gender and all of its blows. Here, I have weaved through the barbed passageway of my teenage desires again, have made a trek out of my ancient wants. Oh, to be a girl once more, who in 2014 watched keenly as her tutor sat atop his desk and splayed his legs outward while she bit her lip across from him. In my hankering for him then, I made him large and pure. I took him to be a kind of handsome demiurge. My lust for him turned him exemplary, a man who could do no wrong. In his hankering for female students, of which—over the last decade—there have been a small handful, he made me small and expendable. This, I think, is where the great sullying lives. This, I think, is how my pain moves and travels, in that it did not come into existence when the two of us first met in the classroom a little over ten years ago. Nor did it unfold when he admitted, one afternoon, to having invited another student into his bed. Or another.

It pulsed in the everyday sexism of being made woman. There it was, between the credits of every raucous noughties sex comedy I'd seen growing up, where women were prescribed little more than a wet T-shirt and three cocksure lines. Male desire, such as this, decides us throwaway. All sex, and little more than that.

This pain is so simple, it feels almost elementary. The thing is, I had once felt special. Unique. The exception to the rule. The condition of my specialness, of being the idiosyncrasy in my once-upon-a-time-tutor's budding career, of having lost my footing and fallen squarely into his lap by sheer coincidence, was imperative. Mandatory, one could say. And now instead I am bestowed the wobbly outline of a cliché I don't stand by. I have, in due time, become the rule. This is because here—in the institutional playground of male desire at its most banal—there are no exceptions. I just didn't know that then.

In writing this book, I have exhumed many a ghost from its resting place. I can feel these wraiths, skinned and small, as they sidle out from my grip. They want to be left alone, too. Through Blaine, Cara, Rose and Elsie, I vowed to return to myself at nineteen, just to see. Perhaps that's what this book is about. How women, at various junctures of their lives, will be forced to reckon with the kind of love they, as girls, once laid out a warm mat for. They may have lit candles then, or burned incense sticks, or simply coaxed their wants from beneath some marled rock without even a flame, just the hum of their sweet voices. We arrive at ourselves eventually. We are, after all, the honest descendants of our once girlish rituals and will shake ourselves clean of their promises in due time.

RESOURCES

If you or anyone you know is in need of support for mental health concerns, help is available, 24 hours a day, seven days a week, anywhere in Australia.

Lifeline

24-hour crisis support

13 11 14

lifeline.org.au

Suicide Call Back Service

1300 659 467

suicidecallbackservice.org.au

1800RESPECT

National Domestic Family and Sexual Violence Counselling Service

1800 737 732

1800respect.org.au

National Student Ombudsman

Current or former students can lodge complaints with the National Student Ombudsman.

1300 395 775

nso.gov.au

In an emergency, call 000.

ACKNOWLEDGEMENTS

To Kelly, for your solidarity, your tireless companionship and your dogged insistence on my mission.

To Gabriel, for your endless support, for the cards on the wall.

To Mindi, for the memes.

To Fil, for remaining the most sacred thing that slipped through the cracks.

To Brigid Mullane of Ultimo Press, for your trust and encouragement, as well as Sophie Mayfield and Elena Gomez for your considered, generous edits.

To every woman who reached out, eager to share their story. All of it matters.

Madison Griffiths is a writer, artist and producer based in Melbourne. She is the co-producer of *Tender*, an award-winning podcast that follows what happens in the aftermath of abusive relationships. Her essays have been published widely in *The Guardian, The Age, The Monthly, The Saturday Paper, Vogue, Meanjin, Marie Claire* and more. In 2022, she won the Our Watch Award as administered by the Walkley Foundation for Excellence in Reporting on Violence Against Women and Children.